JEWISH SPIRITUALITY

IN THE SAME SERIES

JEWISH SPIRITUALITY

SARA ISAACSON

Thorsons
An Imprint of HarperCollinsPublishers

Thorsons
An Imprint of HarperCollins*Publishers*
77–85 Fulham Palace Road,
Hammersmith, London W6 8JB

The Thorsons website address is: www.thorsons.com

Published by Thorsons 1999

1 3 5 7 9 10 8 6 4 2

© Sara Isaacson 1999

Sara Isaacson asserts the moral right to
be identified as the author of this work

A catalogue record for this book
is available from the British Library

ISBN 0 7225 3731 X

Printed and bound in Great Britain by
Caledonian International Book Manufacturing Ltd, Glasgow

CONTENTS

Grateful thanks to Andrea, Dahna and Meital Katz
of Jerusalem for their vital help and information

INTRODUCTION

The spiritual core is the deepest centre of the person. It is here that the person is open to the transcendent dimension, it is here that the person experiences ultimate reality.

RABBI ARTHUR GREEN

This book is about Jewish spirituality. Its aim is to show the relationship between the practices and ideas of Judaism and the underlying spiritual bedrock on which they are based. Thus it will not provide you with a handbook on Jewish ritual – although anyone wanting to know more about what goes on throughout a Jewish life will learn the essential details here. Nor will it enlighten you on how to become a Jewish mystic, even though reading it may give you insights into the mystical experience. What it does is interweave all of these, demonstrating the inner significance which runs consistently through the outer structures.

What is proving not so easy in the modern world is how to form a living connection between the religious culture you belong to and your inner spirit. Organized religion is often derided as being devoid of inner wealth – sterile, rigid and authoritarian, a modern irrelevance. Attachment to religion may be justified pragmatically in terms of cultural tradition, personal identity and community support. Religion as providing transcendental experience or spiritual sustenance, though often sought, is uncommon.

Religion has this century lost popular esteem. It is often suspected of causing wars and conflicts, of being the source of political strife and personal anguish. Yet there is still hope it can be redeemed. Many people are turning anew to religious practice – with a difference. What is new is a desire to see inside religion's external surface and feel the heart of its spiritual impulse. Recently the spiritual quest has turned towards Eastern religions, with reworkings of Buddhism and Hindu philosophy admixed with Judaeo-Christian myth and ideals to form 'New Age' beliefs and practices. In this contemporary blend, many people have found something that speaks to them. It has helped make sense of times of crisis and verified the conviction that 'this' world is not all there is.

The new formulae have also revealed the gap left by conventional religion. People are waking up to the fact that it is not providing for modern needs. Yet for many who do belong, no matter how tenuously, to a religious tradition there is a nagging feeling. Perhaps, buried in the depths of habit and repetition and mumbo-jumbo, what you need is available precisely in your own roots.

MODERN NEEDS, AGE OLD ANSWERS

Jews everywhere are re-examining their own religious tradition. There are growing numbers of *baale tshuva* – people returning to orthodox practice. Contemporary movements such as Reform and Conservative Judaism, Masorti and Modern Orthodox are aiming to make conventional religion more relevant to this day and age.

Others are doing Judaism their own way, creating a 'New Age' Judaism. In the words of Reb Zalman Schachter-Shalomi, a leader of the Jewish Renewal movement, 'Jews everywhere are on a quest motivated by a malaise, a feeling that there must be more in Judaism than the cut-and-dried version frequently encountered in contemporary services. The seeker [is] in search of a way to express spiritual stirrings, and a practical method with which [to] develop that holy source within so that it will begin to flow freely.' People in the Renewal movement meet in small groups for prayer and discussion, often reworking the ritual in accordance with their group needs so it becomes more meaningful.

Other Jews throughout the world are simply looking at what it is to be Jewish, formulating their own relationship with Judaism. In Eastern Europe, Judaism more or less became eradicated or went underground in the aftermath of the Holocaust and Communism. Now there is an unprecedented flowering of interest in Jewish philosophy and practice, a pride in and desire to affiliate with Jewishness. And many entirely secular Jews are still aware of having a Jewish core which generates its own unique outlook.

Why is all this happening right now? A few decades ago thought and action were dictated by those around us. Now we no longer submit unquestioningly to communal and religious order, but are encouraged to work it out for ourselves. We have all become free-thinkers, our belief systems stemming from personal experience rather than communal ideal. This individual expression can often leave us without overall direction. The drive towards personal development is being grafted onto eternal needs – a profound belief system, answers to anguish, the encounter with joy – that are real food for the spirit.

There is thus a need for a redefined spirituality which fits the disconnected individual. In Judaism there is a particular impetus to seek. Jews are aware they are part of an age-old tradition

with intrinsic truths that have endured for centuries and sustained generations. It is hard to locate the living spiritual tradition in a religion with strongly entrenched practices and rituals like Judaism, but many people feel it is worth trying. For many Jews there is a growing sense it is the only place to look. For those born outside the Jewish tradition, too, the heart of Judaism can bring inspiration. It is for all these people that this book is written.

It should be mentioned here that notwithstanding the variety of new appraisals and ways of 'doing' Judaism, this book describes largely the normal practices of traditional Jewry. While all of the more recent developments of Reform, Liberal and other movements have a place and meet a need, looking at Judaism's unchanging elements, rather than its innovations, seems to be the best place to start unfolding the deeper foundations on which it has grown.

SPIRITUALITY – WHAT IS IT ANYWAY?

The dictionary says that spirituality is 'opposed to matter, concerned with the sacred or religious, not concerned with external reality, proceeding from God, holy, divine, inspired, to do with higher qualities'. It is important to differentiate it from religion, termed 'belief in superhuman controlling power, the expression of this in systems of faith and worship'. It is also useful to distinguish mysticism, as 'seeking unity with the Deity, believing in the spiritual apprehension of truths beyond understanding, to do with the hidden, the esoteric'.

An ultimate scheme of the transcendental, then, might look something like this:

RELIGION
Religion is any belief system which stands at the jumping-off point from the tangible world of everyday things.

The belief system must include a God or gods – the idea of some superhuman force which is beyond what we can see and touch. This being, entity or force helps control our world and our lives in an interactive universe. Religion also includes certain practices which accompany this belief system, helping manifest it as a reality in the practical world.

SPIRITUALITY

Spirituality is everything that has to do with whatever is not transient.

It is to do with the world which we cannot see but which we somehow apprehend, without necessarily comprehending it. It ties into religion in that religion is essentially spiritual since it is to do with what is unseen. It is also an essential foundation for mystical practice.

MYSTICISM

Mysticism presents a further development from religion and spirituality.

It is to do with direct appreciation of the unseen world or worlds – a knowing on a different level. Traditionally, mysticism is based on stringent upholding of religious belief and practice. These must work together with esoteric ritual to bring about a direct experience of the Divine universe. Mystical experience, though often longed for, is not for the faint-hearted – it can bring about powerful 'altered states' and classical Jewish sources warn against it unless you are adequately prepared.

While we can talk fairly concretely about religion and spirituality, mysticism is more difficult. For one thing, mystical experience is always highly subjective and loses a lot in translation. Secondly, in the Jewish mystical tradition there are constant reminders that such things are not to be spoken of – although this did not stop mystics attempting to communicate their experiences. Although all three components are to do with supra-reality, talking about the spiritual meaning within Judaism is not necessarily an introduction to the mystical path. Fascinating and attractive, and a genuine seam within the Jewish tradition, mysticism is essentially about personal entry into a very different dimension – the revelation of the innermost secrets of creation.

That said, mysticism has always had an influence on mainstream Judaism. While the heights of mystical experience are the prerogative of the few, there are few areas of normal Jewish life which are not imbued with ideas which have infiltrated from Jewish mysticism. Even the Jewish liturgy contains strong elements of mysticism, which have become incorporated into it and are largely unnoticed by mainstream synagogue attendees.

'POPULAR' SPIRITUALITY – THE SOFTER WAY

'Spirituality' is fashionable in a way that 'religion' has lost. While 'religion' carries implications of being boring, dutiful and moralistic, 'spirituality' has a softer feel. It has about it more of the impulse of the heart, relevance to the individual soul. It is more to do with inner connections than external impositions, with personal ways of being than adherence to ritual activity.

Ultimately the spiritual has become associated with the core within that can connect up with the part of cosmic reality not normally seen nor materially experienced. It may be felt as a bridge between the religious impulse and mystical illumination, and many of us today find it more of an inspiration than normative religion. In Judaism, though, the stress is always on the foundation stone of practical religious action as a precursor to spiritual experience and perhaps even the encounter with the presence of God.

ANCIENT IDEALS, NEW TERMINOLOGY

There was no such word as 'spirituality' in Jewish tradition before medieval times – comparatively late in Jewish history. In many cultures today there is still no separate expression for the spiritual. While in current Western usage the term implies an opposition to worldliness, the first use of an equivalent word simply referred to philosophical and scientific concepts. The medieval Kabbalists, who were very much immersed in the path of mystical Judaism, developed 'spiritual' as a term in its own right, but by this they meant a religious ideal which came from an amalgamation of ancient Hebrew and Greek thought.

It is easy to speculate that for ancient man, sacred time and space – just concepts to us today – were once so real that a separate terminology for them was unnecessary. Now, perhaps with growing awareness of the inner dimension of the individual soul, we find it important to name the spiritual in its own right. It has become real to us not as something concrete, but nevertheless as a definable intangibility in our lives.

However spirituality is understood today, we can say that it is influenced by the Hellenistic and Christian worlds which acknowledged the personal and individual. Hence 'spiritual' has sometimes become a buzz-word for inner feeling, internal sensibilities.

In its Jewish context, though, it helps to reflect back on the sense of original non-separation, when the sacred was natural. Segregating 'spirituality' from Jewish practice and thought is an unnatural deconstruction. Judaism often seems a religion of strict law and custom. In fact spirituality is integral but often buried in all that ritual – thus the practice has been accused of taking over from feeling. It is also important to recognize that in

XIV

Judaism 'spiritual' does not necessarily isolate the inner, personal experience which it has come to signify. For practising Jews, the intellectual concept, the knowledge of God's world, is as important as the experience of the heart.

SPIRIT AND PHILOSOPHY – AN EASY ALLIANCE

We tend to think of spiritual principles as perennial, inherent and unchanging, while philosophical concepts are subject to fluctuation. In fact in Judaism the two are so interlinked that their only constancy is a state of flux. There have been vast influences on Judaism throughout the ages, and new ideas have always been introduced and absorbed. When scholars sought to define and rework Judaism they did so according to their own bias, the culture of the time and place in which they lived.

This has in turn affected Judaism's spiritual outlook. As ideas have been integrated into the religion, its inner being has developed too. It is as though the soil of Judaism, which is made up of core components, can still be turned over, examined and reordered. While this basis remains intact, there is constant movement around it in terms of both the intellectual and spiritual.

It is this which can perplex outsiders – how can Judaism be at once so rigid, so entrenched in tradition, and yet also embrace change? Judaism has always been subject to a ferment of debate and analysis. There are also many kinds of Judaism, some tolerant and flexible, some bound to the unchanging ways of the past. The answer is that Judaism can be all these things yet more. Those who believe change is the lifeblood of Judaism are as much part of the fold as those who hold fast to fundamental principles.

PRINCIPLES OF JEWISH SPIRITUALITY

Is there a particular sort of Jewish spirituality, different from all the rest, and how can it be distinguished? If spirituality has to do with the intangible foundation of religious practice, then Jewish spirituality is different by its association with Jewish practices. Judaism is known for its practicality, for the many commandments which practising Jews carry out. Their spiritual value is linked inextricably with them.

Judaism does have a unique spiritual outlook, differing in essentials from other major religions. Martin Buber, an important interpreter of the Jewish mystical philosophy Hasidism, has pointed out that in Judaism each soul serves God's creation, irrespective of any aim for itself. In contrast, Christianity has more to do with the fate of the individual soul, its personal salvation in eternity. Christians also believe that faith in Christ is necessary for redemption from original sin – an idea rejected by Judaism, which emphatically states that we are born unflawed but choose constantly whether our life is to lean towards good or evil. Essentially, too, Judaism believes that no human being can *be* God, but each can work towards emulating God's ways.

Contrasting too with Eastern spiritual ideas, traditional Judaism has never believed in becoming perfected in a way that transcends the ego and the limitations of this world. The quest is more to find out what God wants and to be obedient to his will to ensure continuance of the people and to establish the Divine on this Earth.

In particular, Judaism expresses the idea that God is to be drawn into the world of man, a theme particularly stressed in the medieval *Kabbalah* and later in the Hasidic movement. Thus, the relationship between God and man is a two-way process in which the spiritual can be helped to find a place in the world as well as man find his place in Heaven.

Linked to this process of continuing interaction is the fundamental concept that it is possible to find closeness to God in all things. Again, Judaism has its own view on how this is done. Universalist concepts state that everything which seems (to our unenlightened eyes) to be mundane is really spiritual. Judaism prefers to conceive of God as being at once not here – very separate and different – yet also imbuing the world we experience with his being. Thus the world is very definitely *not* God, but of God.

In Judaism we always have an active part to play. Judaism does not rely on a spontaneous experience of spirituality. It requires us to do certain things in order to see in a certain way. Thus, the spiritual does not settle upon one. Elusive yet reachable, the spirituality in Judaism is let in by your actions in this world.

SIGNIFIED BY SYMBOLS

Judaism has a ban on direct representations of God, so a structure has grown up in order to represent and put us in mind of what we cannot see directly. From the Star of David to the seven-branched candelebrum, symbols have powerfully brought to life the shape of Jewish spirituality. At its most intense, we have the bizarre imagery of the *Kabbalah*, with its *sefirotic* structure based on the qualities of (or emanated by) the Divine being. This is often represented as the Tree of Life.

There has always been something in Judaism to link us imaginatively and with great creative power to the spiritual universe. Whether ascending to the spiritual world or helping it descend to the human one, Jewish spirituality is a living dynamic process.

PART I:

SPIRITUALITY IN THE STORY OF THE JEWISH PEOPLE

The Jewish people have been bound together for something like 3,000 years. While other civilizations have come and gone, the Jews have persisted – usually quite against the odds. This part of the book explores the varied history of the Jewish people, looking at it not just as an unfoldment across time but also assessing the underlying threads which have contributed to the Jews' survival.

In a sense these can be seen as spiritual threads, because they are hardly those of practical reason. What has preserved the Jews has been intangible – more faith than logic, trust than action. There has been very little that Jews have been able to hold on to in material terms. Instead, survival has relied on what is not at all part of the tangible world – a spirit kept within their midst.

Throughout the centuries Jews have defied all neat categories. This too has resulted in a sort of resoluteness, because if a people cannot be defined in narrow terms, they can escape extinction when they lose a particular way of being. There have been times when the Jewish people were the greatest political nation of their area – the biblical era of the great kings. Losing all that, they became exiles for the first of many times in a strange land, without king or country. Re-establishing themselves, they became a strong religious force with a central Temple rebuilt and rituals intact – only to have to reformulate their entire religious structure and practice when that physical centre of religion was destroyed, seemingly forever. Without land and structure, the Jews had to evolve into different forms and those depended on the circumstances in which they found themselves. Externally, then, they found a variety of ways of being defined – as a religion, a people, a nation. All of them overlapped and were subject to prismatic reconstruction according to how they were perceived.

But it was internally that the Jews found their strength and sustenance. A mixture of ritual and belief, ways of life and attitudes of mind kept them anchored in something unique and particular. The ability to take their spiritual soil with them also allowed them to grow and persist, whatever the outside world might try and do.

TIMETABLE OF MAJOR EVENTS IN JEWISH HISTORY

BC

*c.*2000	Start of period of the Patriarchs – Abraham, Isaac and Jacob
*c.*1280	Exodus from Egypt
*c.*1200	Settlement in the land of Israel
*c.*1125–1050	Period of the Hebrew Judges
1020–1004	King Saul
1004–965	King David
965–928	King Solomon
928	Splitting of the kingdom in Judah and Israel. Reigns of various kings
720	Assyrians capture the kingdom of Israel. Ten tribes taken into captivity
586	Destruction of Jerusalem by the Babylonians. Exile in Babylon
538	Return of the Jews to Israel from the Babylonian exile
520–515	Rebuilding of the Temple
458–428	Period of Ezra and Nehemia
332	Alexander the Great conquers Israel; Hellenic period begins
219–217	Seleucid period begins
167	Hasmonean rebellion begins, resulting in independent Hasmonean kingdom
*c.*38	Herod the Great begins rule

AD

First century– early fourth century	Roman rule in Judaea (now called Palestine)

4	70	Siege of Jerusalem, Temple destroyed. Jewish Diaspora begins
	132–135	Bar Kokhba rebellion
	First century–sixth century	Rabbinic period
	c.210	*Mishnah* edited
	325	Start of Byzantine period. Christianity dominates Western world
	c.390	Jerusalem *Talmud* completed
	c.499	Babylonian *Talmud* completed
	640	Rise of Islam
	942	Death of Saadiah Gaon
	1096	Start of the Crusades
	c.1100	Start of the Golden Age for Jews in Spain
	1105	Death of Rashi in France
	1141	Death of Judah Halevi in Spain
	1182	Expulsion of Jews from France
	1204	Death of Moses Maimonides in Egypt
	1290	Expulsion of Jews from England
	c.1291	Death of Abraham Abulafia
	c.1296	*Zohar* completed
	1492	Expulsion of Jews from Spain
	1496	Expulsion of Jews from Portugal
	1498	Immigration of Jews to Poland begins
	1572	Death of Isaac Luria in Safed
	1609	Death of Judah Loew in Prague
	1623	First Jewish settlement in America
	1648	Cossack massacres of Jews in Poland/Lithuania
	1656	Jews readmitted to England
	1665	Shabbetai Zevi claims to be the Messiah
	1760	Death of the Baal Shem Tov in Poland
	1786	Death of Moses Mendelssohn in Berlin
	1797	Death of the *Gaon* of Vilna
	1831	Judaism granted equal status with other religions in France

1833	Beginning of the emancipation of Jews in England
1848	Emancipation of Jews in Germany
1881–2	Start of wave of major pogroms in Russia and mass emigration of Jews
1882	Beginning of Zionist immigration to the land of Israel
1894	Dreyfus trial in Paris
1897	First Zionist Conference takes place
1917	Balfour Declaration says Jews should have the right to a national homeland in Palestine
1935	Start of anti-Jewish legislation in Germany
1943	Last Jewish ghettos in Europe destroyed, transport of European Jewry to death camps
1948	Birth of the state of Israel; War of Independence begins
1967	Six Day War in Israel; Jerusalem reunited

IN THE PRESENCE OF GOD

And all the people perceived the thunderings, and the lightnings, and the voice of the horn, and the mountain smoking; and when the people saw it, they trembled, and stood afar off. And they said to Moses: Speak thou with us, and we will hear; but let not God speak with us, lest we die. And Moses said, Fear not, for God is come to prove you, and that His fear may come before you, that you sin not ... And the Lord said to Moses: Thus thou shalt say unto the children of Israel: Ye yourselves have seen that I have talked with you from heaven.

EXODUS XX, 17–18

The source for the spiritual traditions of Judaism has to be the Bible. The relationship between the Jewish people and the Bible has always been special. The first five books of the Bible – the *Torah* – are read in weekly portions throughout the year, giving Jews the chance to explore and re-examine the familiar texts. It is in this connection that the Jews are called the 'chosen people'. Often misinterpreted as an expression of self-importance, the term more correctly means being chosen for a particular sort of responsibility. This responsibility involves listening to God, taking seriously the commands and obligations laid down in the Bible and finding out what God wants you to

8   do. Every Jew therefore needs to know what leads to the true
spiritual life and the biblical texts are the foundation which
informs both the heart and the intellect.

This intimate relationship with the Bible thus also involves a
special relationship with God. The concept of Yahweh, the one
God, set the early Israelites apart from the surrounding Near
Eastern cultures and their polytheistic religious beliefs. Previously the assumption had been that human beings were at the
mercy of a whole variety of gods, whose loves and wars governed the state of the world. The monotheistic idea provided a
concentration of power where everything was invested in one
being. Having just one God altered your world view. Instead of
reflecting the human condition of variance, with adventuring
gods doing what they would, the Israelite God fostered a sense
of supreme order. Most important of all was God's code of
behaviour, which he gave to the Hebrew people. Following it
gave them a hand in their own destiny, difficult though it might
be to bring God's world into the human one. The ancient
Israelites were in no doubt about who ruled the world. They
also had to find ways to work with the will of this great being.
The sense that an order might be possible, and seeking ways to
achieve it on Earth, is the essence of this new relationship with
the one all-powerful force.

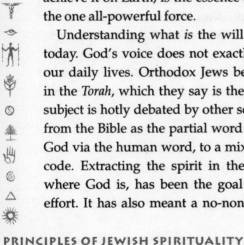

Understanding what *is* the will of God is problematic to us
today. God's voice does not exactly ring out loud and clear in
our daily lives. Orthodox Jews believe that it is clearly heard
in the *Torah*, which they say is the actual word of God, but the
subject is hotly debated by other sections of Jewry. Views range
from the Bible as the partial word of God, as being inspired by
God via the human word, to a mixture of story, myth and legal
code. Extracting the spirit in the scriptures, finding out just
where God is, has been the goal of much Jewish intellectual
effort. It has also meant a no-nonsense approach to the Deity.

Since the biblical period Jews have been berating God as much as he chastises them. Sorting out God's real voice and requirements is not just a matter of being obedient and deferential – it means arguing and wrestling as in a dynamic real-life emotional relationship.

God's word may be hard for us to discern, but the direct sense of God's presence was there for the Jews of the biblical period. The texts show that God, real or perceived, was experienced as being among the people. They felt his involvement in every activity. There are many references to this experience of God. At times it came through specially chosen individuals such as the patriarchs or the prophets, at other times the whole community of Israel knew that God was with them. Some people believe God's voice *was* physically heard, simply because there was less interference, and if you 'tuned' yourself, as the Jewish people were attempting to do, you became a stronger reception vehicle, much like receiving a good radio signal. Whatever our present-day interpretation, God – benevolent, angered, challenging or forgiving – is seen as an ever-present force in the events of both personal and communal life.

God's direct presence is said to have withdrawn after the last destruction of the Temple in Jerusalem and will not be experienced again until the Messianic Age. Yet although this direct 'line' to God no longer exists in our day and age, we are expected to look back to those inspirational times and draw from them. Retelling the story allows us to put ourselves in the place of those who did hear the voice of God and to see what we need to do today.

HEARING THE PRESENCE – WHEN GOD'S VOICE WAS CLEAR

Certain key biblical events form the cornerstones of Judaism. Their stories are recounted to children in religious school, they are a central part of the liturgy retold in the synagogue. Did they really happen? Historians, archaeologists, rationalists and fundamentalists will probably argue the case for and against until the end of time. What matters is that the biblical stories comprise the mythology of Judaism and are part of the Jewish national consciousness. They are both religious lore and creative force. It is in these age-old tales that God seems to speak most forcibly, confirming his presence and making us aware of another dimension, powerful, pure and directly accessible.

THE CREATION

The story of the Creation which begins the Bible is the first of the weekly *Torah* readings. In Hebrew it is called *Bereshit*, which literally means 'in the beginning' and is also the Hebrew title for the whole Book of Genesis. The story is eloquent yet beautifully pared down to the utmost simplicity. God, the prime cause of all things, creates out of nothingness by means of his voice – 10 'sayings' which have been the source of huge and varied interpretation. Ideas about the word of God range from taking it literally to perceiving the 'voice' as a mysterious creative force, in the sense of an energetic vibration or a sound wave. Yet somehow order appears out of chaos, in the presence of one Divine being.

The Jewish interpretation of the story also sees the God-like possibilities in mankind. Although related to the animal world, man is separated from it. The difference is consciousness, enabling us to be partially of God's realm.

The Creation story is simple yet mysterious. Judaism has always been curious about its anomalies. As one example,

Heaven and Earth are created, yet water, which is divided on the second day, seems to be already there. What starts as a series of bald statements is already creating tension. The story asks you to explore it, find explanations. It provides Jews with a fundamental dichotomy. As a starting-point the Jewish people must accept God as the prime mover in the universe. From that point, you are free to delve deeply into God's moves and motivations.

The Creation story has also withstood changing ideas about evolution. In one way a primitive myth belonging to ancient cosmologies, it is not completely out of step with current science. A second Creation tale (Genesis 2:4–25) presupposes a certain amount of created universe already in place – a second stage Creation coming out of the first. One initial dramatic event – a kind of 'Big Bang' – thus leads to further evolutionary process. The Genesis story seems to move with the times, above all rationale, fixed yet fluid, simple yet with endless possibilities of interpretation.

THE PATRIARCH

Abraham, the first of the Jewish patriarchs (the others are his son Isaac and grandson Jacob), is – so the Genesis story goes – called upon by God to travel to 'the land that I will show thee'. Without further ado, at the age of 75 he takes his family from Haran (in present-day Syria) and obeys the command to trek to Canaan. Obedient though Abraham is, this kind of undeliberated action may also fill us with horror. In Abraham's case there is more to come. He is asked to take his only son, Isaac, born according to God's promise in the extreme old age of both himself and his wife Sarah, to a place of sacrifice and to make a burnt offering of him. The totality of Abraham's obedience is spine-chilling. At the moment of the ritual slaying of Isaac, God's voice gives a reprieve and a ram is sacrificed instead.

The story of Abraham is utterly central to Judaism. Its force lies in the way Abraham's motives are presented. His obedience is not that of the flawed human being, misled by *naïveté* or madness. His story is about supreme faith. We can conceive of this as total surrender, letting go of personal will and desire. Yet Abraham shows an even higher possibility for mankind. He is part of the human race, yet his actions are unquestioningly attuned to the will of God. Abraham reveals the possibility of being at one with God. His story has sustained the Jewish race.

THE LEADER

Moses is the spiritual leader *par excellence* in Judaism. He is known as the greatest prophet, the lawgiver, the first Rabbi and teacher. He is most famed for bringing the Jewish people out of Egypt where they had been forced to work for the Pharaohs after famine made them leave the Israel of the patriarchs. In the biblical story Moses leads the people through the Sinai wilderness to within sight of the Promised Land. His reception of the Ten Commandments at Mount Sinai and the people's acceptance of an everlasting covenant forms the Jews into the community of Israel.

The Exodus from Egypt occurred some time around the thirteenth century BC. There are no contemporary historical documents recording the Pharaohs' ill-treatment of the rapidly increasing band of foreigners in their midst, as recounted in Exodus 1, or of the eventual decision by the hard-pressed leader (said to be Rameses II), visited by a succession of plagues, to let the Israelites go (Exodus 12). Again, though, we are dealing less here with historically verifiable events and more with the reality of the myth in the history of the Jewish people. Traditional Judaism does not doubt that Moses existed and was extraordinarily close to God and at times in direct contact with him. More questioning Jews take Moses as a figurative leader, a symbol of God's direct revelation. Esoteric ideas about Moses also say that he spent years in the desert in training to become a high priest, developing the powers necessary to lead his people to freedom.

However he gained it, certainly the legendary Moses has a power which enables him to hear God's voice and transmit it to the Israelites. He can part the Red Sea, allowing the Israelites to cross to freedom, he can strike a rock in the desert to bring forth water for the thirsty people. Yet these actions are not intended to show Moses' prowess – rather, they demonstrate the presence of God.

In all this, the Israelites are constantly discontented. They are the voice of everyday common consciousness, which focuses on material well-being and loses sight of the spiritual. Moses must constantly remind the people of God's presence. He provides manna which appears miraculously each day, he leads the way by means of a cloud which is in front of them by day, a pillar of smoke at night. Moses is the leader who keeps the people in touch with God. As a real man of God, or part of the Hebrew mythology, Moses and the story of the Exodus go down in Jewish history as passionate examples of freedom from oppression, trust in the face of suffering and the coexistence of human vagaries and the Divine will.

Yet Moses has a fatal flaw which makes him more credible. Spiritually unique, his actions are expected to accord with the high power invested in him. For showing a moment's doubt, he is not allowed to enter the Promised Land, but dies before his people come out of the wilderness of Sinai. Moses thus shows the unlikelihood of complete spiritual attainment – the main task is to live in the knowledge of God even when failing to emulate him.

THE PEOPLE

The moment when the Israelites became a people is said to be when Moses brought the Ten Commandments down from Mount Sinai. The Israelites were not permitted to go up the mountain with Moses, 'lest they break through unto the Lord to gaze, and many of them perish'. Only Moses, through his priesthood, was protected enough to be able to look on the face of God. This idea persists throughout Judaism. Direct connection with God is not for the spiritually unprepared.

While Moses was the only one allowed close to God, what happened at Sinai was the revelation of God to the people. Standing far off, they nevertheless experienced the Divine presence more completely and dramatically than at any time before or since.

In order to withstand the strength of God's presence, the people were required to prepare themselves spiritually for Moses' return from the mountain with the Divine message. Their purification process, which included sexual abstinence and bathing, was a ritual sanctification which prepared them in mind and body for meeting God. A strict barrier was also put on the mountain from which Moses descended, making it a holy place of particular power.

The idea of Sinai and the revelation is central to Judaism. While God revealed himself in his message, it was also the choice of the people to accept the Commandments and in doing so to enter into a covenant with God. This contrasts with other religions of the time, particularly the Egyptian religion, which was a body of Mysteries entrusted to priests. The Exodus from Egypt, signifying the breaking away from the old myths, culminates in the taking on of new religious precepts which have now also become a moral and spiritual code for the Western world. Particular to Judaism, though, is the covenantal idea. God commands, but the people must agree to take the commandments on board and continue to renew that agreement.

Yet in the biblical account, the covenant is immediately broken. The people lose faith in Moses and in God and worship instead a golden calf, an idol of their own making. The spiritual once again struggles in the face of human behaviour – loss of faith, the return to old habits, cynicism and disapproval. But all is not lost. As a result of Moses' intercession, his direct pleading with God, a kind of dual atonement is created. Surprisingly, the atonement is on behalf of God as much as that of the Israelites. Asked by Moses to 'repent' of his anger, God's forgiveness is as essential to the covenantal process as the repentance of the erring tribe. In Judaism return to God is always possible, even after dire transgression.

LAW AND REGULATION – THE CODE FOR LIFE

The Bible is a profound interweaving of history and fable, guideline and faith. Many people think that 'dos and don'ts' and a few mythical stories are all there is in it. True, reading the third book of the Bible, Leviticus, you are presented with a detailed mass of requirements relating to the Israelites at the time of their wanderings in the Sinai desert. Yet these requirements also regulate the lives of Jews today.

The Book of Leviticus deals primarily with the intricacies of keeping intact a priesthood and a priestly nation, which is what the Israelites had become after accepting the law at Sinai.

THE CREATION OF PURITY – SANCTIFYING SACRIFICE

Leviticus says a lot about sacrifice and goes into rich detail over the gamut of animal offerings which the religious ritual of the time entailed. This emphasis on animal sacrifice can embarrass modern sensibilities. Are Jews really expected to

dwell on this period and, even more, hope to return to it?

Animal sacrifice was finally abandoned when the central Temple in Jerusalem was destroyed by the Romans; tradition says that we cannot return to the rituals without the rebuilt Temple of the Messianic Age. Whether we return to sacrificing animals, therefore, is a moot point and not one which many Jews would regard as a real possibility – more probable is that in such a future age, the spirit of the sacrifice but not its physical reality would be retained.

It is difficult to put ourselves in the place of these remote ancestors whose religious ritual took from surrounding cult practices which were then the norm. It is also quite possible that animal sacrifice was a departure from human sacrifice. Whereas traditional sources insist that Judaism arose as a completely new phenomenon with a high spiritual and moral framework, the truth is that the Israelites were very much part of the surrounding world of their time. Unique though they may have been in disowning previous traditions, they were still largely informed by them. Worship in the ancient world was unthinkable without sacrifice.

What was different, however, was a closer meaning in the individual's response to God by way of the sacrifice. The great medieval Jewish philosopher Maimonides pointed out that sacrificial worship became spiritual during the development of the Jewish ritual. Rather than being a means of performing magic, that is, seeking influence with the idol, animal sacrifice became a way of expressing a personal relationship with the one God. So a burnt offering would not just be surrendered to appease a god; it would be the expression of your self-surrender to the will of God. A peace offering would be a symbol of gratitude for God's mercy, not just of hope that the god would see fit to smile down upon you. And the important congregational sacrifice kept alive the sense of a national consciousness, the sense that the Israelites were one people responsible to one God. All of this formed the basis for a more internalized variety of religious consciousness in which the individual self had duty and responsibility – an intervening consciousness, if you like, between the previous pagan gods and the forces of nature.

The accounts of animal sacrifice describe the intricacy with which the ritual had to be performed and the power invested in it. This ritual's purpose was to ensure absolute purity. There could be no room for mishap either in the animal in its original state or in the way in which it was slaughtered and offered up. Ritual was precise, intense and the only way to provide a real sense of communion between the people and the force of the Divine. Giving up life, spilling blood, were serious and sanctified practices. Ultimately, as in Day of Atonement (*Yom Kippur*) ritual, the whole people would become purified and spiritually renewed as a result of the sacrifices made by the priest on their behalf.

MORE THAN TEN COMMANDMENTS

Purity is the focus of the second part of the Book of Leviticus, which deals with the holiness of the people of Israel. This holiness could only be fully reached through complete adherence to the commandments (*mitzvot*), which were said to purify the whole of life.

The Rabbis of the post-biblical era considered Chapter 19 of Leviticus to contain the essence of Jewish law. This relates to the time when the Jewish people were forming as a nation and their religious ritual was becoming fully developed. It reiterates the Ten Commandments in greater detail and gives other injunctions to separate the Israelites from the customs of surrounding peoples. It is not just the Ten Commandments, then, Jews must adhere to. From Leviticus the later Rabbis evolved a complex system of regulations which still rule Jewish life.

The laws governing a Jewish life are fundamental to all religious Jews. They cover every conceivable human activity from getting up in the morning to eating and praying and sexual conduct *(see Part II: Spirituality in the Life of a Jewish Person)*. The ones that are best known – to both Jews and non-Jews – are the laws of *kashrut* (literally, the fitness of the food you eat) and of *Shabbat*, the day of rest.

The original spirit which formed a people out of a wandering tribe came from following a set of laws given for the whole community. Yet as well as these laws, Judaism offers guidelines which make it an all-encompassing way of life. Ultimately, the whole of the *Torah*, the first five books of the Bible, can be seen as being concerned with separation. It brings alive the ancient concern with keeping the Jewish people apart and making them aware of their identity.

GOD AS PRESENT – THE PORTABLE TEMPLE

After the revelation at Sinai God's dwelling-place came to be considered the Sanctuary (or Tabernacle), containing the Ark of the Covenant, which was built to be carried around by the wandering Israelites. The Ark was in the chamber known as the Holy of Holies, the inner sanctum of the Sanctuary. The Sanctuary became known as the *Shekinah*, originally meaning God's dwelling-place, later his spirit on Earth and later still his feminine aspect. It is also sometimes called the Tent of Meeting because the entire wooden framework was covered by a tent.

The building of the Sanctuary occupies a large part of the Book of Exodus and the construction details are very precise, right down to the types of metals, wood and materials used. Mystics have interpreted it as symbolizing the universe in its completeness and complexity – a model, if you like, of the macrocosm. Maimonides said that the Sanctuary formed a home for the religious ritual and that these together helped shape the Israelites as a people before they had a spiritual home, enabling them to keep the sense of God permanently in their midst.

Much has been written about the Ark of the Covenant. Esoteric theories have deduced that it was some kind of force field and there may be an element of truth in that even though we have no way of knowing just what kind of power the Ark did contain. In much the same way that the Israelites were enjoined not to get too near to God on Mount Sinai for fear of losing their lives, the Ark had certain constraints put around it and was dangerous to be near unless you had performed the correct protection rituals. When it was being taken towards Jerusalem at the time of King David (shortly after 1000 BC), contact with it killed an attendant, Uzzah, who had reached out to keep it steady.

We cannot possibly know just how the Ark received its power. The Bible suggests it was simply the reception vehicle for some vital element of the Divine spirit. It is also possible that ritual and faith invested it with power, so that the belief of the observer actually created a particular effect.

The static structure of the Temple was built to house the Ark in Jerusalem during the reign of King Solomon, which began in 965 BC. The idea had been first mooted by King David, but he did not live to see his dream become reality. Instead, Solomon completed the lavish structure with its chambers and pillars, candles and incense, altars and carvings, which was to become the place of pilgrimage for Jews from all over the land and allow them proximity to their God and a sense of intimate connection with him.

The Temple was momentously destroyed by the Babylonian army in 586 BC, which was tantamount to the Israelites' world coming to an end. By this time the Ark had disappeared from biblical accounts – its resting-place forever to be a cause for speculation.

The Temple's remains lay in ruined Jerusalem until 520 BC, by which time the Persians had overtaken the Babylonians and the new king, Cyrus, had sanctioned the Jewish return to the Holy Land. The rebuilt Temple, however, was neither sumptuous nor impressive and there was no Ark to set at its centre. Now God had become truly spiritualized – without a corporeal home, a being of thought and imagination. The Temple, continuing as a place of ritual, remained as a holy reminder, and the purity of the buildings and those who worshipped there was still sacrosanct.

Under Hellenism, the expansion of Greek culture from around 300 BC, the Temple came increasingly under attack, but it was left to the Romans under Pompey to occupy and thus finally violate it in the year 63 BC.

A last and glorious attempt to reinstate the Temple was made by Herod, the vassal king of the Jews, in 19 BC. Of marble and gold, this splendid sanctuary drew huge amounts of pilgrims for the three great festivals, Passover (*Pesach*), the Feast of Weeks (*Shavuot*) and Tabernacles (*Sukkot*). But it could not sustain the volcanic political climate of the Roman Empire. Jewish zealots fought to the last defending its sanctity, but the Roman army dealt its last destruction in AD 70.

While the Ark and the Temple (which became synonymous with the Sanctuary) were physical realities at the time of Solomon's Temple, their symbolic force became real after its final destruction and the dispersion of the Jewish people. They embody the idea of taking God with you, of God being in your midst. This idea is essential to the formation of the Jewish spirit before entering the Promised Land. It powered the building and rebuilding of the Temples in Jerusalem, and it sustained Jews

when the Second Temple was destroyed in Jerusalem and the
Jews dispersed. The idea has thus become multi-dimensional.
On one hand, Jews pray for the rebuilt Temple, the physical
structure which is bound up with the hope for a perfected universe. On the other, there is the reminder of the once physical
core of Divine power, moving with the people as they travelled
through the wilderness. Between them both is what has become
present reality – a symbolic image of an enduring yet mobile
presence, of being able to set up a home for God on Earth wherever you may be.

THE COVENANT IN ACTION

> In thee, O Lord, do I take refuge; let me never be ashamed: deliver
> me in thy righteousness. Incline thy ear to me; deliver me speedi-
> ly: be thou my strong rock, a fortress of defence to save me. For
> thou art my rock and my fortress: therefore for thy name's sake
> lead me, and guide me.
>
> PSALM 31, 1–4

When the Jewish people experienced God's presence at
Sinai, they formed an agreement to become a community subject to the laws brought to them by Moses.
These people who entered the Promised Land after wandering
in the desert were a diverse bunch. Rather than being made up
of one unified group which had formed in Egypt, they appear to
be partly people already in the area, partly a group from Sinai
with whom they joined forces. This community then formed its
identity around the treaty with God.

Although this idea of an agreement with a higher force may
well have drawn inspiration from contemporary political agree-
ments, it grew to signify more than just practical protection,
becoming a metaphor for the joining of the Divine and the
human. It enabled the Israelites to disassociate themselves from
the magical practices of foreign cults, particularly Egypt, and

to form themselves into a people with a powerful force of their own. The Israelites thus started life in the Promised Land, Canaan, with the unique bond of a holy covenant.

This exclusive worship singled out the people from those around them. As the Israelites gradually settled the land under their early kings and held onto it, even through declining rulership, until their exile in Babylonia (the ancient Mesopotamia and present-day Iraq and Iran), they retained and fostered that sense of being a unique people.

Later, on returning to the land from Babylon, where they had been as it were displaced from the presence of God, the scribe Ezra exhorted them to go back to true Temple worship – with all the sacrifices intact – under the law of Sinai. The tradition of exile and return became entrenched in the spiritual history of the people and has an enormous hold on Jewish consciousness today.

The years to come saw a constant attempt on the part of the Jewish people to redefine themselves. They stood fully in awe of the *Torah*, becoming more sensitive than ever to the possibilities of being exiled and the necessity of developing rituals for staying close to a God who would allow release from external bondage. As time went on they defined themselves as separate and protected their contract with God. A spiritual commitment to the laws of Sinai resulted in a practical way of life which rejected whatever might interfere with their own self-preservation.

THE SPIRITUAL IN VERSE

Many people feel that the most spiritually moving part of the Bible is the Book of Psalms. This has been considered a spiritual text in its own right and Jewish people will often recite it or part of it on Sabbaths or festivals. The psalms are traditionally attributed to King David, who has become entrenched in the national

memory as a figure of great wisdom and literary prowess rather than just a political leader. However this belief was questioned from early on by the Rabbis of the post-biblical era and remains unsolved today.

Some of the psalms are known to be very ancient, dating from before the destruction of Solomon's Temple in 586 BC. Scholars believe that they may well have originally been an integral part of the religious liturgy rather than poetic literature. Many psalms have an essential quality of either praising or petitioning God, which may have had more to do with the sacrificial rite than an expression of individual emotion with which the psalms are associated today. It is likely, then, that our concept of the psalms has altered over the centuries as the words became separated from the sacrificial worship.

After the Temple's destruction, when the Jews were taken captive in Babylonia, the psalms began to enshrine the hopes and dreams of a people cast out, far away from the centre of their spiritual existence. New psalms were added at this time and these had more in common with wise sayings and exhortations. The psalms became an inspiration in their own right, a necessary adaptation to changing times.

Perhaps more than any other part of the Bible, the psalms have the ability to appeal to the changing needs of their readership. When we need the words for praise, the voice for supplication, the guidance to get us through daily life, the psalms are our easiest resource. Connected to antiquity and symbolically linking us with a great Jewish leader, they still seem to speak right from the modern heart.

KINGS AND HEROES

Jews look back to the time of the great kings with a special longing. The great biblical heroes are legendary names yet they are also fallible human beings. Saul, the first king of Israel who expanded the territory, was prone to depression. David, who reigned after his death in 1010 BC, was at one time a close intimate of Saul's but was forced to flee when Saul became overcome by jealousy of him. Stories about David show his many changing faces. He was a musician and a poet, a conqueror who established the rule of the Jewish God in Jerusalem and had a legendary love affair. He is idealized as a great king despite his human failings. King Solomon came next. An adept military man, he is famed in mythical memory for his wealth and wisdom, even though under his rule the kingdom began to show the first signs of disintegration.

These heroic figures are a mixture of political strength, emotional reality and psychological frailty. They may be great leaders, heroes, but they are also men, not myths. Judaism's giants all have an earthy humanity and create the sustained idea that to be spiritually in touch with God is not just for saints, but also for those who struggle and fail.

PROPHETIC JUDGEMENT

Priests and prophets occur throughout the Bible. They ring warning bells, they sing of God's glory, they convey messages of apocalyptic doom and they ensure the people never forget their God. The prophets are said to be imbued with a special power, marking them out from ordinary human beings. This power is the hallmark of the spiritually developed man with an intellect so clear that further development, that of extra-sensory function, is able to come into being. The prophets see with a clarity that connects them to God's purpose, in order that they may transmit it to the rest of the people.

Prophecy in ancient Israel was a way of keeping the people mindful of God's purpose. It saw God's will unequivocally in

26

everything. Essentially anti-mainstream even when they belonged to the ruling establishment, prophets quickly criticized monarchs and priests when they considered the essential covenant with God was being demeaned. The prophet Elijah, active in the first half of the ninth century BC fought a solitary battle to ward off the Baal worship of surrounding nations. The eighth-century prophet Amos issued warnings against social injustice. He was the first 'literary prophet', leaving writings about the fight against oppression and reminding the people that theirs was a covenant which freed the poor. Isaiah, one of the prophetic 'greats' and another literary figure, continued this tradition. Berating the people for their evil ways and for forsaking their God, he prophesied the coming of darkness and a Messianic Age. Isaiah had elaborate visions of God, 'upon a throne, high and lifted up', surrounded by *serafim* (a high order of angelic beings). He was a passionate spokesman for the urgent need to reform and come back to the knowledge of God.

Jeremiah, whose name is forever associated with doom and gloom, had reason for his forebodings. He began prophesying the destruction of the people in 627 BC and indeed during the next 20 years there was considerable political unrest with threats from both Egypt and Babylonia. Jeremiah attributed this breakdown to Divine anger at the sins of the people, who would be chastised for 70 years. Indeed, Jerusalem fell soon after his premonitions began to be taken seriously. He also spoke more optimistically of the importance of turning against evil. Validating his insights, the foundations of a new Temple were laid within 70 years after the destruction of the first, although its walls were not to be dedicated until 445 BC.

The powerful voice of Ezekiel, who came to Babylon with the exiled Jews in 586 BC, was crucial to the times. His vision of the throne of God in all its splendour inspired the exiles. For them God needed to be pictured and described in order to be kept in the mind and heart. Ezekiel's vision was also the main-spring of later mystical activity, as mystics aspired to experience directly the Divine world he so vividly described. Ezekiel had other visions too, such as that of dry bones which are resuscitated at the End of Days into human form. This imaginative reality created the spiritual sustenance the desolate exiles needed.

Prophets acted as a wake-up call. When the people were lethargic, they warned of the dire results of their laxity. When the people became demoralized, they reminded them that God was still in their midst. They taught not personal salvation, but communal obligation – God's relationship to the chosen people was through formalized agreement, not personal whim or shifting circumstance. They were messengers from God, holding the people to their commitment – to trust, to obey and to remain faithful.

WELLSPRINGS OF MYSTICISM

The mystical movement in Judaism, which gained ground as a phenomenon in its own right from the first century BC, is rooted in the Hebrew Bible. Certainly there were esoteric groups in Israel during the time of the Second Temple, the Qumran sect being one of the most interesting because of the wealth of information about it conveyed by the Dead Sea Scrolls.

Mysticism had a different impetus from the traditional discussion of biblical texts which the Rabbis who emerged in the aftermath of the dispersion held so dear. Mystics were concerned with a personal revelation rather than the public and communal experience of God as witnessed at Sinai. More, the revelation experienced by the mystics was not limited to one time and space, but could be repeated so that the nature of the Divine world could be clearly accessed. It has been suggested that the prophets were themselves great mystics with the ability to focus powerful spiritual force.

Two particular passages in the Bible have been a major influence on Jewish mysticism. One is the story of the Creation in Genesis. The second is the first chapter of Ezekiel, where the prophet has his vision of the throne of the Deity. Both of these have been the subject of much exposition and speculation. Exploration of the 'works of Creation' (*Maase Bereshit* in Hebrew), especially, was supposed to be an esoteric secret and its ways were not divulged. Fortunately for us, however, mystics did discuss and record their experiences in great detail.

It is not hard to see why these two areas were of special interest. Both give perhaps the closest insights into the inner mystery of God himself. They are like windows into the direct nature of the Divine world and by focusing on them with the use of esoteric techniques for changing consciousness the mystics did everything they could to align themselves with God himself.

REVOLT AND CHALLENGE

The Jewish people are famed for their survival. During the Classical period, with a history of at least 1,000 years already behind them (more if you include the mythical origins in the time of Abraham), their solidarity was to be challenged by both Greek and Roman expansion. Hellenistic culture spread Greek ideas which many Jews found attractive. Eventually a full-scale revolt was launched by Jews loyal to the Jewish way of life against the encroaching Greek culture and Seleucid kingdom of Syria, the current political overlords.

The Revolt of the Maccabees, begun in 167 BC, led to the last glorious rule in Jewish history – the Hasmonean kingdom, established in 140 BC. It was, however, still impossible to get away from Greek influence. Vigorous attempts were made to keep Jewish tradition intact and the functions of the monarchy and high priesthood both came under attack for demoting God as the true ruler.

The last great military challenge came during the Roman Empire.

The last great military challenge came during the Roman
Empire. The destruction of the Temple had as its aftermath the
beginning of the end of Jewish sovereignty. Finally the Bar
Kokhba revolt, starting in AD 132 and continuing for three and a
half years, showed that the Jewish spirit and consciousness
were still alive.

The revolt failed to displace Roman rule. It marked the end of a
Jewish national entity and the beginning of an entirely new order
of Jewish life. Martyrs of the wars, committing suicide in the
name of God, became legends in the Jewish consciousness.
Spiritual strength had come from within. Without land, dispersed and decentralized, there had to be new ways of surviving.

RABBIS AND TEACHERS – THE WAY OF THE INTELLECT

The way the Jewish people found now was to do with drawing
on past tradition and formulating an intense and complex code
to live by. Formerly, with wave on wave of political unrest in
Palestine, they had been subject to diverse forces which had led
to wide differences over what Judaism was all about. One of
these forces was to grow into fully-fledged Christianity.

The Rabbis who arose at the start of the first millennium,
then, had two main tasks. One was to secure the link with God
in the absence of God's presence in the Temple. The other was
to unify the people as a community in the face of external influences, particularly the wildfire spread of the new religion which
had Christ as its spiritual centre.

The first five centuries AD belong to the great sages of Jewish
memory. They gathered the whole Jewish oral tradition into the
Mishnah – a complete code of Jewish life. Further clarification of
the *Mishnah* resulted in the *Gemara*, and the two works together
became the vast tractate, the *Talmud*. As well as this, the

Rabbinic sages evolved a whole body of literature commenting on and interpreting every area of Hebrew scripture. These included expositions of the intricacies of law (*halacha*) and a creative and imaginative genre stories around biblical texts, known as *Midrash* and *Aggadah*.

This codification of Jewish practice does not simply tell you what to do. It is a record of deliberation and debate. The whole process of teaching, discussion and dissemination kept God alive, though the method was different from anything ever done before. Cult ritual based on unquestionable faith was gone for good. Now the aim was stimulation, the involvement mental. Communities began to be based around teachers. Intellectual controversy raged. Above all, interest was maintained. This period of Rabbinic literature laid the foundation for a mental connection with the mind of God.

A BETTER FUTURE

Does the Bible have anything to say about a spiritual future? Inherent to the biblical message is that the world is a receptacle for ultimate redemption. The biblical prophets, particularly, emphasize the idea of a Messianic Age.

This prophetic message about the future arose naturally out of the conditions of the times, where a cataclysmic end to the people of Israel was a distinct possibility at any time. It is, however, rather vague. God is expected to speak and the End of Days to be announced, but this has little to do with an individual figure or saviour. The House of David will be restored (this idea still has emotive qualities for the Jewish people) and the glory of Israel will return. There will be everlasting peace and all nations will turn towards the God of Israel and give up heathen cults. 'From Zion goes forth the *Torah* and the word of the Lord from Jerusalem.' The vision reflects a Utopian ideal

fostered by ancient religions looking to their former age of glory
now lost.

This vision, however, formed the basis for a complex attitude
to the future of the world and indeed a personal future after
death which was developed later. Notably, the mystical tradition extrapolated from the biblical ideal and cultivated a defi-
nite Messianic fervour, which variously came out into the open
and went underground with the claims of false Messiahs. Traditional Judaism has taken the biblical idea rather more cautious-
ly, concentrating on maintaining Jewish law and observance
and allowing that the future redemption, when the word of God
will be heard by all people, will happen in some far distant
future and in its own good time.

MEDIEVAL SPIRITUALITY

God, may His mention be exalted, wished us to be perfected and
the state of our societies to be improved by His laws regarding
actions. Now this can come about only after the adoption of intellectual beliefs, the first of which being His apprehension, may
He be exalted, according to our capacity. This, in its turn, cannot
come about except through divine science, and this divine science
cannot become actual except after a study of natural science.

MOSES MAIMONIDES

The medieval period spans a lengthy area of Jewish history. It runs from the rise of the Moslem world – around
AD 600 – until roughly 1,000 years hence, AD 1650.
Throughout this time the Jewish people were spread out among
many and different nations, and subject to the sweeping influences of both Islam and Christianity.

Key features of this period were the dispersal of the Jews
away from the Near and Middle East, where they had largely
been concentrated, and their adaptation to the societies which
admitted them.

It is impossible to make an overall summary of Jewish fortunes during this time. Jewish life was characterized by change
and constant reformulation according to shifting circumstances.

Its most remarkable feature is the unwavering persistence of a Jewish spirit and identity.

The force of religion was central. The medieval world was unthinkable without a religious orientation. Unlike today, religious life was not an individual matter of personal choice, and your religious allegiance governed everything from your social status and legal obligations to your central concept of life and death. It was also a time when philosophy was pursued as a way of finding truth and was, therefore, deeply bound up with religious thought. The legacy of the Greek philosophers such as Aristotle and Plato influenced both Moslem thinkers and the Christian world. Philosophy was a spiritual search for understanding God's ways and the purpose of human life. Philosophical debate thus enriched religious thought whilst supporting or disproving the religious systems of the time. While serving God was generally held to be the central aim of life, how best to do so was hotly contested.

The Jews were in the thick of this. Visible now in many areas of society, they were also problematic. A phenomenon of interest as the original people of the Bible, they had also rejected all further revelation – and were, therefore, unacceptable. Adhering to their own little world yet at large and dispossessed, they were objects of both suspicion and veneration.

In the highly charged intellectual fervour of the medieval period people sought to know and understand as well as believe and do. Learning and discussion caused changes within Jewry as well as in its relationship to the outside world. Judaism had to become rationally based, to stand up to dissemination and examination. Its survival was based on evolving a tight internal structure of thought and behaviour – and accepting the status of a wandering people, at the mercy of religious and political change.

After the momentous destruction of the Jerusalem Temple in AD 70, the Jewish people were effectively left without a spiritual home. Many in fact stayed in the vicinity of the Temple, despite the ravages of war. Rabbinic wisdom continued to be gathered and spread out from centres of learning within the Holy Land, but the spiritual reality of a sanctified place was in ruins. Instead, it had to go within. From that time on the Jewish people created an internalized spiritual home. The ritual forces that had kept them in touch with God had now to be translated into means employable wherever they were. That meant turning sacrifice into prayer, pilgrimages into festivals, and every Jewish home into a place where God could live.

This reorganization of the Jewish spiritual framework enabled Judaism to survive down the centuries. Demographic change and upheaval were to be the order of the day right up until the present. In many places Jews lived creatively and successfully, with the liberty to function as a separate people in adopted lands. Yet they were always subject to the whims of the powers-that-be. Centuries of tolerance could be brought to an abrupt end and a thriving Jewish presence eradicated almost overnight. Instead of rooting themselves in their own soil, then, the Jews took up their soil and travelled with it.

A central force in the new formulation of Judaism had to be Rabbinic rule. The emphasis on Rabbinic thought and legalistic writings meant a great deal was now invested in the power of the Rabbi. In their capacity as leaders and scholars at the great academies (*yeshivot*) of Jewish learning, Rabbis would send directives throughout the Jewish world expounding on a point of law. Rulings evolved relating to every aspect of Jewish life. As time went on and Jewish demography changed, customs could vary considerably from place to place. In particular, the ritual which came to be known as *Ashkenazi* (the Hebrew name for 'German' but actually a blanket term for Jewry which spread westwards from the Near and Middle East to Italy, France and Germany) became quite different from that of 'Oriental' Jewry (*Sephardi*). What mattered was that a central authority would generate a way of doing things throughout whole communities of Jews, with the focus on maintaining the link with God that Temple service once provided. Each aspect of Jewish life now had to be scrupulously and punctiliously defined so as to replace the connective power of the Temple ritual.

Where did the Jews congregate on their dissemination from the Holy Land? Babylonia had been a home to them since the exile of the sixth century BC. Many remained there and were able to continue autonomously under changing rulership, to be joined and revivified by Jews fleeing the land of Israel in the early centuries of the first millennium. Babylon provided great centres of Jewish learning for around 15 centuries.

Jewish life also spread to the Byzantine Empire (now Turkey, Greece, Cyprus and Bulgaria), where attitudes were ambivalent under Christian rule and more tolerant under the Ottoman Empire from the fifteenth century AD.

European or *Ashkenazi* Jewry grew gradually and at random through the second half of the first millennium. By the start of the second millennium communities of Jews were known in parts of Italy and throughout France and Germany. In fact many had probably lived there since the Roman Empire. Jews lived in England from the time of William the Conqueror until they were evicted in 1290, and France followed suit. In Spain Jewish life had various flourishing periods, from Roman times to the Moslem conquest in AD 711 and later, culminating in a 'Golden Age' for Spanish Jewry. North Africa, also part of the Moslem Empire, became acceptable territory for Jewish settlement as well. Even after Spain became dominated by Christianity again,

Jews still flourished, but during the fifteenth century Jewish life there took a disastrous turn. The establishment of the Inquisition, to root out 'new' Christians or Jews who had been forced to convert under the re-conquista, led to a final calamitous expulsion of Jews in 1492.

Meanwhile the Crusades made Europe increasingly antagonistic towards its Jewish communities. Jews were segregated and subject to legal discrimination, but tolerated where they could be of use to the ruling powers.

From the thirteenth century there was a gradual spread of Jewish life eastwards towards Poland and Russia, creating a flourishing if often persecuted Eastern European Jewry with its own rich traditions and patterns.

The history of Jewish Diaspora settlement is often seen as tragic. But seeing the Jews as a consistently persecuted people is only part of the picture. Between the periods of disruption came stability of a kind, where communities not only adjusted to new countries and conditions but also contributed to them economically and culturally. Externally there was wide cross-fertilization of culture and religion, particularly within the Arab world. Internally the strong structure of life based around study, prayer and customs affecting and governing all areas of life held the people together. Jews were both perceived as being different and felt themselves to be separate. Whether accepted into society or forced apart from it, a special Jewish identity was intact. Whether publicly proclaimed or as a place of silent refuge, the Jewish spirit was shaped by adversity and challenge throughout the medieval era.

MYSTICS AND MYSTERIES

Jewish mysticism has its roots in the biblical period. The period known as 'late antiquity' – from around the second to the early seventh century AD – produced mystical activity of a rather different order. It was largely centred around concepts of the *Hekhalot*, the system of Temples or palaces said to make up the Divine realm, and the *Merkavah*, the chariot that carries the throne of God described in the first chapter of Ezekiel.

The earliest mystics were fired by an absorption with the whole nature of the world of God. They had their own schools, produced a large body of literature (great amounts of it still exist) and were involved in several levels of practice. In a mixture of intellect and creative imagination, there was great speculation on the precise nature of Ezekiel's vision and of the Creation itself. One unique mystical work from this time is the *Sefer Yetsirah*, the 'Book of Creation'. It accounts for the Creation by means of 'mystical paths' – the letters of the Hebrew alphabet and the 10 *sefirot* (the originating cosmic forces), variously representing number, dimension and elements. A highly esoteric weaving of mathematics, linguistics and cosmology, it is the foundation of later kabbalistic works.

But as well as this mental activity, the mystics were intent on their own direct experience of the world which Ezekiel described. They were also influenced by contemporary commentaries on the Song of Songs, nowadays taken to be a beautiful and allegorical love poem dwelling on the union of God and the people of Israel. For the mystics, however, it had more to do with an actual description of the form of God and was a way of establishing a relationship with him.

From early on we have accounts of 'mystical ascents' into the Divine realm. These were brought about by the kind of esoteric practices known to mystics of most traditions, such as fasting and the repetition of sounds (chanting), in order to bring about what we would call 'altered states of consciousness' or trance-like states. This would give the mystic the ability to separate his spirit from his physical body and gain access to the realms of God.

These states are well authenticated, not just in the esoteric literature but also in classic Jewish texts. The *Talmud* itself contains the story of four Rabbis who performed an 'ascent of the soul' into an Eden-like garden or orchard. It is a kind of warning, recounting that only one, the well-known and revered Rabbi Akiva, survived the journey, since he was pure enough in spirit to sustain the presumed energetic charge of the direct presence of God. The others all came to unfortunate ends – dying, going insane or 'cutting down the shoots' (possibly committing heresy).

Other esoteric literature tells of more successful journeys. The Book of Enoch deals with the transformation of the man Enoch, who is briefly described in the Book of Genesis as 'walking with God'. He becomes a leader of the archangels with the secondary Divine power of assisting God in creation. As the recipient of Divine knowledge he views the exact nature of the palaces of God and knows the powers of God throughout the cosmos.

The mystical world views revealed by this super-charged set of literary accounts show on one hand a wide range of contemporary cosmological speculation on how God and his leading associates create and power the universe. They also give insight into the whole variety of magical and esoteric practices employed by people who wanted to go further than the ritual activities of Jewish legal requirement.

It is hard to know how far the mystics adhered to strict Rabbinic doctrine. Study of the *Torah* as carried out by the Rabbis was the acknowledged method of knowing God and God's ways. Observances, although highly ritualized, were expected to be done in full awareness of their connection with God's purpose. Yet there were many alternatives to this mainstream. The Qumran sect, a highly esoteric group dating from around the start of the first millennium whose activities are known to us through the Dead Sea Scrolls, was certainly stricter than the norm in its ascetic practices. We simply don't know what part the early mystics played in the Jewish community. Neither do we understand their relationship to the Rabbis of the time and whether attributing mystical experience to well-known learned men was just a means of validating the stories. But an intense search for spiritual experience beyond the norm was clearly a major feature of the times.

THE SPREAD OF THE INTELLECT

The medieval period's philosophical ferment was not just a matter of dry intellectualizing. It was a rigorous search for religious truth. Jews had their part to play in all this and the great Jewish philosophers were not only influenced by ideas from the surrounding cultures but also able to leave their mark on mainstream thought.

Rabbi Saadiah Gaon, who lived from AD 882 to 942, is known as 'the father of Jewish philosophy'. He was the spiritual leader of one of the great Jewish academies in Babylonia and his ideas were revolutionary. Spiritually and philosophically, the times were confusing, with many religions and philosophical systems vying for predominance. Additionally, the Karaite sect was threatening Judaism from within. The Karaites believed that only the bald biblical injunctions should be followed, rather than the more legalistic but people-friendly Rabbinic ones. Saadia Gaon spoke against their controversial insistencies, which would have meant a much stricter and joyless religiosity. He offered inspiring answers to the conflicts of the times, discouraging religious doubt and reconciling the new knowledge of science, logic and astronomy with Rabbinic Judaism. In line with current thinking, he offered a rationalistic explanation of Judaism's traditional concepts instead of resorting to informal polemic, as had been Judaism's only defence until then.

Other great Jewish philosophers include the poet and mystic Judah Halevi, who lived in twelfth-century Spain and explained the intricacies of Jewish thought to interested outside observers. His book, *The Kuzari*, attempted to give an explanation of the Jewish faith. Also against the background of Moslem culture, the twelfth-century thinker Abraham ibn Daud gave the case for maintaining faith along with philosophical reasoning.

Religious writing also flowered in eleventh-century France. Rabbi Solomon ben Isaac (Rashi) was a great intellectual whose commentaries on the *Talmud* are still acclaimed today. He fused a literal interpretation of biblical and Rabbinic texts with creative explication. He also wrote in the light of the times, attempting to maintain the Jewish perspective against Christian reworkings of texts used to persuade Jews to convert. Followers of his Talmudic commentaries, the *tosefists*, set up schools of study with rigorous intellectual standards. But they also made the methodology of disputation and analysis, which had invigorated Jewish thought in classic Talmudic tradition, stand up and be noticed by the outside world. These commentators also infused Jewish life with the vigour and self-worth to withstand the horrors of the Crusades.

One of the most illustrious Jewish sages was Moses ben Maimon, the twelfth-century scholar Maimonides, who is still revered today. He was born in Spain, and lived in Morocco and Egypt, where he was court physician to the Sultan. Maimonides set himself the huge task of trying to make Judaism's emphasis on faith appeal to those influenced by the new philosophy of reason. He had a rigorous philosophic approach, which has caused him to be regarded as a strong rationalist. Additionally, he wanted to ensure that the now exceedingly complex system of Rabbinic law should become understandable and meaningful to all. He acted as a spiritual guide throughout the Islamic Jewish world.

In a way Maimonides fell between two stools. Although highly authoritative, his work was condemned by traditionalists as being too open to heretical philosophical ideas. It was also felt that he played down Judaism's central items of faith and the mystical stream in favour of excess rationalism. The conflict was bitter yet it also revitalized Judaism. No longer could it be inward-looking, dispersed and left behind. The controversy reached all areas of the Jewish world, forcing examination of attitudes towards the nature of Jewish faith and how it could be sustained and explained.

HIGH KABBALAH – THE INVENTIVE PHASE

The second phase of Jewish mysticism is the area dominated by *Kabbalah*, which literally means 'reception'. *Kabbalah* is fashionable today because it represents the non-intellectual, legalistic stream of Jewish thought and allows the creative use of spiritual feeling.

This wasn't, however, always the case. *Kabbalah* really has two separate streams of development. One attempts intellectually and symbolically to define the cosmos and its workings. The other concentrates more on mystical method and practice. Both came out of early mysticism, where there was both a whole system of thought about what the Divine world was like and the attempt to experience it personally through the ascent of the spirit. The intellectually-based system of *Kabbalah* developed from speculative writings such as the *Sefer Yetsirah* (Book of Creation) and carved the way for the *Bahir* (Brightness), an esoteric work which appeared in Provence around 1170. It talks about the nature of the *sefirot* – the originating cosmic forces – and formulates them into a structure not just involved in the initial Creation but also in constantly charging the universe.

42   The best known piece of kabbalistic literature is the *Zohar*, the
'Book of Splendour' which first appeared in thirteenth-century
Spain. The *Zohar* has misty origins, like all these esoteric works,
which were hotly debated even then. It was said to have been
written down by Moses de Leon under the spiritual guidance of
a second-century sage, Rabbi Shimon bar-Yokkai ('channelled'
as we would call it today). Moses de Leon himself said he
copied it from an ancient manuscript but others suggested
he made it all up himself.

These mystical writings seem to us today highly imaginative.
They are a journey led by poetic allegory, with a language of
their own suggesting the complex world which is God's realm
but is also capable of being known by human beings. This
world, to the Kabbalist, is governed by the *sefirotic* structure,
now evolved into outpourings ('emanations') of God's spiritual
force. God himself is acknowledged to be unknowable – called
Ein Sof, 'Without End'. Yet the Kabbalists were not content to
leave him as the distant philosophical entity which rationalism
was turning him into. They were intent on creating a personal
relationship with him. To do this they evolved ways of understanding aspects of his being and the *sefirot* now became identified with these. Closest to the unknowable God himself is *keter*,
the crown, followed by *hokhmah* (wisdom) and *binah* (understanding). Balanced underneath these are *din/gevurah* (judgement and might) to the left and to the right *hesed/gedulah* (mercy,
greatness or loving kindness). These are followed in descending
order by *tiferet* (splendour or beauty), then *hod* (a combination of
power and majesty), and *netsah* (triumph and grace). These two
can sometimes be found in a pair with *hod* to the left. Finally we
have *yesod* (foundation) and *malkhot* (kingship). It is this arrange-
ment that became known as the 'Tree of Life'. Its superimposi-
tion on the shape of the body could also give insights into how
these qualities might interact in the human and Divine realms.

The relationship between the *sefirot* – explaining it, finding metaphors for it and keeping it in a state of harmonious flow – was the mystic's life task. Familiarity with the *sefirot* could only be achieved through intensifying traditional means – prayer and study.

Kabbalists were highly learned in *Torah* tradition, but keeping all the commandments was only the first step. Like the early mystics, they believed there was a world above and beyond that of normal experience which could be reached as long as you were prepared to withdraw to some extent from ordinary life. This would lead to the release of the imaginative, intuitive faculty where extra perception brought you close to God.

Mysticism thus often bordered on asceticism and the *Hasidei Ashkenaz*, German pietists, a twelfth and thirteenth-century sect, came closer to this than most. They would put themselves through physical penances combined with stringent religious discipline in order to heighten their spiritual life. Their practices were like those of Christian monks and martyrs, and in common with them the Jewish pietists believed that to reach God it was necessary to negate all human desire.

More common centres of Jewish mystical activity from the twelfth century onwards were northern Spain and southern France, and later Italy too. *Kabbalah* there became a complex system based around the *sefirotic* idea.

Additional systems of belief developed relating to God's manifestation in the universe, largely through a system of permeation then withdrawal of light. God is therefore in contraction and distant from this universe, yet also experienced by the spiritual force that is left in diluted or reflected form.

Kabbalistic theory also very much involves the human being in the act of creating and recreating the universe. In common with physics, it postulates that everything is in a state of flux. Yet this state is ultimately controllable through correct disciplines

44   aimed at manipulating it in accordance with the will of God. So
we have a part to play in assuring that balance is kept between
the various *sefirotic* elements and also in keeping the flow open
between this world and God. The world we inhabit is in a universe separate from that of the Divinity, yet the two share the
same fundamental structure and are thus closely related. The
mystic in this form of *Kabbalah* – which scholars have termed
'theosophical' or 'theurgical' – is essentially involved in the cosmic structure and able to influence it.

Kabbalah is also in sympathy with modern ideals in that it
conceives of a feminine principle within the Deity. The *shekinah*,
in classic Rabbinic literature meaning 'the dwelling-place of
God', came to symbolize in medieval *Kabbalah* both the female
aspect and the abode of the soul. This does not mean, however,
that the female found acceptance in Jewish mysticism, in contrast to the classic worship of a male God. The *shekinah* has an
ambivalent part in kabbalistic symbolism, often representing
exile and banishment. Not necessarily on account of its own
female power, this idea had more to do with the sin of Adam
which led to the splitting of masculine and feminine. The
unity of the two – God and his *shekinah*, male and female, the
upper and lower worlds, became another focus of the mystical
enterprise.

Practical *Kabbalah*, also known as ecstatic *Kabbalah*, was the
second and ultimately lesser strand of kabbalistic development.
It emphasized practices over and above theories. It was influenced by the Islamic world, especially Islam's mystical stream,
Sufism. The emphasis was on solitude or separation from the
world, repetition of sounds associated with the name of God
and the longing and heartfelt desire to cling mystically to God.
This system also developed methods – impossibly complex to
us today – of mentally visualizing changing combinations of
Hebrew letters. The letters were of great importance because

of their powerful part in the Creation (as when God spoke them in the Genesis story). This was a kind of active meditation which kept the mind charged and extremely concentrated until an explosive change in consciousness was achieved.

The main exponent of this form of *Kabbalah* was Abraham Abulafia, a wandering mystic born in Spain in 1240 who left many writings detailing his experiences of light and God's presence by using these literally mind-blowing methods which are lost to us today. Partially these practices resurfaced in the 'practical *Kabbalah*' of seventeenth and eighteenth-century Poland, where repetition of 'magic' names, chants and the use of amulets with inscriptions of Hebrew letters were used by 'wonder-working' Rabbis for healing and altering people's fortunes.

Over the years, the developments of 'theurgical' (now traditional) *Kabbalah* became more mainstream. Many highly acclaimed Rabbis were also mystics. Kabbalistic groups became well known as part and parcel of Jewish communities and Kabbalists came increasingly into contact with each other and the community through Diaspora movements. Usually they were accepted by virtue of their strict observances, although they were also prone to attack for their innovative ideas.

The extent to which Kabbalists exposed their experience has been controversial. Mystical methods were supposed to be kept underground – they constituted a highly specialized form of knowledge requiring commitment, discipline and isolation and they led to spiritual power. Mysticism was never therefore considered suitable for the untutored masses. Some degree of jealousy and superiority also came into the picture, as well as the belief that the knowledge acquired by the mystics should be available to all Jews. However mystics have always had the dual desire to keep their experiences secret and to publicize them – thus we are left with considerable material about their activities and thoughts.

COPING WITH DISASTER WITH INNER LIGHT

The medieval period was rife with disaster for the Jews. Integration into high society in Spain was interspersed by periods of misfortune under changing Moslem and Christian rule and the final end of the Golden Age of culture and letters after the expulsion from Spain in 1492. Conversion, at one time an answer in Spain and Portugal, enabled whole communities to go underground, keeping up Jewish practices in secret, but this was no longer possible when the Inquisition rooted out these 'New Christians' too.

Likewise, the waves of the Crusades, beginning in 1096 and lasting throughout the twelfth century, spread terror throughout European Jewry. The period of renewed persecution and expulsion lasted until around 1520. Where Jews were commercially valuable they were tolerated; when they became impoverished, they were expelled. They found they had to spread further and further eastwards across northern Europe until Poland eventually provided a safe haven.

Jewish survival to some extent persisted precisely because of external pressure. Where Jews were perceived as separate they intensified their internal sense of separate identity. The development of a specialized form of life with clear patterns of ritual and observance also kept Jews together as a community. Spiritual leadership was provided by Rabbis, who based their power on learning, study and constant reference to history and to the connection with God. The absence of material power in the form of land and military defence could also be said to have encouraged concentration on internal spiritual power.

When it came to the ultimate challenge, of massacre and slaughter, Jews had a particular viewpoint which contributed to their spiritual strength. This was the concept of *Kiddush hashem*, hallowing the holy name by martyrdom. Even where Jews faced the fact that there was no security or chance of physical survival, they resolved to welcome death and even emulate the zealots of past heroic times by committing mass suicide. Thus the sense of inner belief never weakened and Jewish martyrs felt themselves to be sacrificed in order that the world would eventually see its sins and be set to rights. The perpetrators were seen as the guilty ones in the name of God. Jewish innocence, pride and faith therefore stood intact in the face of external catastrophe.

The Jewish people also drew certain practical conclusions from their treatment. Recognizing that there was little hope of tolerance and acceptance, they evolved strategies for survival. Communities knew it was wise to make themselves useful through economic co-operation where that was possible, yet internal self-determination and leadership were also necessary. In Poland this was developed to a high degree and Jewish communities became self-governing units providing for their own needs.

BAROQUE KABBALAH – THE SPIRITUALITY OF SAFED

In the sixteenth century Jewish mysticism flowered anew in Palestine. It was started by Kabbalists fleeing from Spain, where there had been many important centres of mystical activity. Safed, a small town in northern Palestine, now under Ottoman domination, saw a rapid growth of kabbalistic groups, many of whose members came from families expelled by Spain.

The *Kabbalah* developed in Safed was a complex fusion of areas dealt with by pre-existing kabbalistic groups. It was highly influenced by the Spanish expulsion, which was seen as a tragedy for the Jewish people. One way of dealing with it was

to believe the trauma presaged the coming of the redemption and the Messianic Age – traditionally supposed to be preceded by catastrophe. It was also felt that this major force of destruction reflected the cosmic split already symbolized by the exiled *shekinah*. The Safed Kabbalists felt this was the time to redouble their efforts at aligning the universe, restoring balance and unity to a flawed world. They also wanted to redefine their position on the new rational philosophy which had been taken on board by the Jews yet which had also been used against them. They formulated for themselves a combination of mystical belief and ethical behaviour according to strict Jewish law.

Safed Kabbalists formed groups around leading teachers. They performed acts of penitence reminiscent of former groups, such as rolling in the snow, simulating the action of stoning on their own skin, sleep deprivation, excessive fasting and rising in the middle of the night to pray. In this way they provided themselves with the means of attaining spiritual cleansing, not just for private enlightenment but also for the sake of the whole community.

The greatest force in Safed was the teacher Isaac Luria, known as the *Ari* or Lion. His theories were complicated but also imaginative and creative. He saw the world as a mirror image of God's, with human activity reflecting intimately on God. He struggled to explain the idea of evil and enlarged on the thirteenth-century kabbalistic idea that God must also embody evil. He attempted to combat this problem with the colourful kabbalistic idea of light from an infinite source – God – overflowing through a series of vessels, each one, as it reaches further from the source, containing more and more potential for evil. Luria had a large following. He was said to be able to communicate with the souls of the dead and with the animal and vegetable worlds, and was also credited with the ability to see into people's inner being and other lifetimes.

The Safed school of mysticism was extremely influential. It kept alive the old mysticism which had flourished in Europe and imbued it with new life in the attempt to come to terms with current realities. It emphasized human responsibility for the welfare of the world and the effect of human action on altering and healing the cosmos. From this there developed the idea of *tikkun olum*, healing the world. These ideas had a great influence on the development of later mysticism, in the Hasidic movement. In this sense Safed Kabbalism brought Jewish mysticism into the modern world.

TOWARDS TODAY

> In the Ghetto they were without honour, without rights, without justice, without defence – but when they left the Ghetto, they ceased to be Jews. Yet a man, to be a man, must have both freedom and the feeling of community. Only when the Jews had both could they rebuild the house of the Invisible and Almighty God ... who, as the will to do good, is everywhere.
>
> THEODOR HERZL

The modern period of Jewish history has seen abrupt twists and turns of fate. The mid seventeenth century began the great age of European Jewry, in which the cultural traditions which are still associated with traditional Judaism evolved. It was the time of the great European study houses, where scholars gathered to add to Jewish learning. It was also a time when Jews were largely ostracized and ridiculed by the rest of society, denied rights and freedom and turning inward to their own world. In many places they became ghettoized, closed off and shut out.

This era also saw many changes in the non-Jewish world. The age of Enlightenment in Europe brought ideas of social justice and political reform based on rational philosophy. Once again Judaism had to adapt to changing times and find a way of retaining the seemingly irrational spiritual core while appealing to modern thought and values. The conflict between the enclosed life which guarded Judaism and an emancipated one where the Jewish spirit might be lost was fundamental after the Enlightenment, from the late eighteenth century onwards.

Jews had to cope once again with catastrophe and crisis interspersed with the reawakening of inner light. Across Europe there were massacres in the face of economic hardship and the Jews found themselves the butt of religious persecution in the form of blood libels (where the Jews were accused of murdering Christian children and using their blood to prepare the Passover unleavened bread).

Ever hoping that a time of great tribulation would precede the coming of the Messiah, Jews invested high expectations in a series of figures who claimed they could bring redemption to the world through Judaism. Most famous was Shabbetai Zevi, who lived in the mid seventeenth century and whose ecstatic, ascetic personality caused thousands to believe in him as the true Messiah. Even when Shabbetai Zevi took up Islam under threat of death, many Jews retained a secret belief in him and others like him, believing that they were attempting to redeem the sparks of the Divine by 'descending' into the depths of alien worlds.

The death of the Messianic hope for immediate redemption, though, gave rise to a more forcible attempt to lead Judaism back on to a straight and narrow path of traditional thought and worship, without dwelling on mystical dreams. More detrimentally, it brought a spiritual 'low' to the people whose hopes for a better future had been dashed. This longing was to be rekindled in the Hasidic movement, which taught inner joy and made spirituality real – this time for everybody, not just the esoterically-initiated élite.

Meanwhile the rational ideal was sweeping across Europe from the West. Thinkers like Moses Mendelssohn, who lived in Berlin at the heart of Enlightenment fervour in the latter part of the eighteenth century, sought to bring Judaism into the modern age while preserving strictly traditional observance. His followers, however, were not so bound to orthodoxy and a new reforming movement began within Judaism, with the hope that Jews could now become emancipated in society.

Despite political movements in that direction, it was soon clear that the clock could be turned back. Jews were not so easily absorbed into their surrounding society, despite lip service to ideas of equal rights of all. Nationalism, the new consciousness of the nineteenth century, elaborated medieval anti-Jewish concepts and turned them into something more sinister – racial anti-Semitism. Jews became scapegoats for the ills of society. Yet at the same time the Jewish people began to think of themselves as a nationality, with the possibility of recreating a physical homeland. The Zionist ideal, most famously propounded by journalist Theodor Herzl as a political answer to anti-Semitism, was taken up on an emotional and spiritual basis which finally culminated in the founding of the state of Israel in 1948.

EUROPE – THE SPIRIT IN THE TRADITION

In the pre-modern period, however, life in Europe, for all its religious intolerance and fanaticism, political upheaval and disabling economic legislation, saw the cultural and religious life of the Jewish community go from strength to strength. Poland became the centre of attraction and crowds of young Jews came to the East in order to study at the prestigious new *yeshivot*.

The culture of *Ashkenazi* Europe was a unique meld of legal questioning and mystical philosophy. Jews who evolved from this milieu eschewed the external world which they felt would dilute their Jewishness. Jews from the Sephardi tradition, though, were more influenced by the world outside. Spanish refugees, settled in Italy, were less shielded from their surrounding culture, and the communities of Poland also absorbed new ways through the increased availability of printed material on Jewish law, thought and mysticism. It was never possible for Jewish communities to remain completely cut off and much of their ability to survive came through interacting with the outside world.

Great Rabbis carried on the spiritual tradition in Europe throughout the early modern period. Rabbi Judah Loew, who lived in the latter half of the sixteenth century in Prague, had his own academy of Rabbinic scholarship and became chief Rabbi of Prague despite his somewhat original approach. He is associated with the making of the *golem*, a human figure which had featured in stories of occultists from the earliest Rabbinic times. It was said that those who accrued the right powers were capable of forming this figure through the pronunciation of certain sounds and other rituals. In other words, this was in some way an ability to act like God. *Golem* legends abound in the medieval period and the figure itself is held to have the magical powers of warding off demons and other ills which could harm Jews.

Whatever his mystical abilities, Rabbi Judah knew secular literature well and had debates with Christian priests as well as with Jews who had turned to Christianity. He was certainly a learned Kabbalist familiar with mystical writings and activities. He preferred, though, to do without the obscure language of the earlier Kabbalists and to deal in simple ideas. His own writing shows that he had a feeling for inner religious life and that he saw ritual practice as a way of building a pathway to God. Man, he said, was in a state of potential for self-realization, with the soul like a seed within the human body which he is committed to bring to fruition.

Esoteric activity became highly suspect during this period. The late seventeenth and early eighteenth centuries were fraught times for the Jews and a surge of belief that the Messiah

was imminent was followed by discounting of anything based in such 'superstitious' expectation. The time of the Messiah was supposed to be accompanied by an overturning of tradition – necessary to bring about redemption, but unrequired once the Messianic Age had arrived. Thus mystical activity, associated with bringing that time closer, became linked with possible heresies. Some mystics went underground in the aftermath of the false Messiahs, with their overtones of licentiousness, who came in the name of embracing completely heretical beliefs and practices in order (ostensibly at least) to root out evil by fully experiencing it. Expressions of belief in the coming of the Messiah became problematic and any yearning for the Messianic Age was vague and symbolic rather than immediate and actively pursued. Essentially the spirit of Judaism became focused on the here and now rather than the hereafter and any deviation from strict adherence to Rabbinic tradition was less tolerated.

An important orthodox figure at a time when spiritual leadership was most needed was Elijah, the *Gaon* (spiritual leader) of Vilna, the leading Jewish centre in Lithuania. He lived in the second half of the eighteenth century, shortly after the Baal Shem Tov, the founder of the Hasidic movement *(see below)*, which he bitterly opposed. The clash originated not because of his enmity towards mysticism, but more because of his knowledge of it. The Vilna *Gaon* was exceedingly learned in secular subjects as well as being steeped in the *Torah, Talmud* and Jewish traditional literature. This had always been the only way to advance to initiation in Jewish mysticism. He wrote on *Kabbalah* and developed his own mystical powers to the extent that it was said he could even communicate with Elijah the Biblical prophet. He was a strict ascetic who believed that God could not be worshipped without study and that inner devotion arose from adhering to the law. The Hasidic approach, which did not necessarily require traditional learning, but emphasized inner yearning and simple joy, was anathema to him. It would, he believed, lead to ignorance and transgression.

THE HASIDIC MOVEMENT, SPIRITUALITY FOR ALL

In spite of this, the Hasidic movement is still alive and well today. Its roots go back to eighteenth-century Poland, where it offered a vital and spirited 'alternative' which almost split the Jewish community in two.

The founder of the movement, Israel ben Elieazer, known as the Baal Shem Tov (Master of the Good Name), was one of a number of mystics around at the time. How far he was a scholarly Kabbalist learned in tradition is not known, although he must have had some working knowledge of Jewish law. The Baal Shem Tov's abilities, though, lay more in the field of 'practical *Kabbalah*', the branch of mysticism which used esoteric knowledge for healing and producing spells and charms to allay physical and psychological ills in the community. The Baal Shem Tov also seems to have had charismatic qualities which endeared him to a group which later elevated him as its founder and leader. In particular, he seems to have practised meditation-like techniques such as thought control, the devotional concentration of 'clinging to God' and the 'ascent of the soul', where the physical body is left behind.

After the death of the Baal Shem Tov in 1760 the Hasidic movement spread like wildfire under a series of leaders. It was popular because it suggested that deep spiritual experience lay in the heart of the individual and that it was the attitude behind prayer and observance that provided the transformative factor. Hasidism appeared extremely radical because it seemed to open up a change in consciousness, previously only known to mystics, to anyone who wanted it.

Also appalling to its detractors was its emphasis on one's inner state which seemed to demote the importance of study and knowledge. Actually, inner purity of spirit had always been a factor among mystics, but because the Hasidim seemed to focus on this, outsiders seized on it as evidence that they neglected normal ritual. Their bizarre activities, such as song, dance, smoking and somersaults, provided more fuel for those who said they could not be functioning as orthodox Jews. Particularly problematic, and reminiscent of secret sects, was that the Hasidim segregated themselves off from the rest of the community and altered several factors in the time-honoured prayer ritual. In fact the Hasidim were ultra-exacting on most ritual matters, even to the extent of introducing additional strictures.

Eventually, after almost 30 years of bitter struggle, the Hasidic movement became part of normative Judaism and many of its ideas were adopted into traditional thinking.

Essentially Hasidism is an attempt to allow anyone who wants to pray consciously and to become aware of the manifestation of God in all things. Joy in worship was always paramount, since the Hasidic way is to acclaim the being of God through intense gladness. Story-telling to reveal a spiritual truth is also important. The Hasid is characterized by enthusiastic commitment to performance of each and every commandment – very much contrary to the original criticism. Concomitant with high levels of observance is intense inner concentration on prayer and ritual in an attempt at deep communion with God.

Mystical experiences of the high order known to kabbalistic initiates were part of Hasidism, but not for the common man. The *tsaddik*, the leader of a group or school of Hasids, was usually singled out because of his abilities in this sphere. His followers would gain some spiritual elevation through being in his presence, but were not expected to reach his level.

Hasidism is appealing today because it allows a personal relationship between man and the Creator. It celebrates life (within the traditional Jewish framework) and sees that the glory of the spiritual presence can be experienced here and now. This is not necessarily a way of peaceful, unfolding revelation. Often it is a matter of intense activity, in prayer and in life. To the Hasid, life is a process of both elevating oneself to the consciousness of God and making this world fit for the sacred to dwell in. Hasidism fuses all previous Jewish spiritual movements with its elements of disciplined observance, ecstatic conscious-changing practices and the process of uniting with the Source of all things.

SURVIVING THE ENLIGHTENMENT

The Enlightenment movement which spread across Europe in the latter half of the eighteenth century promised to allow Jews to enjoy the privileges of 'normal' life. Jews themselves, particularly in Germany, where the Enlightenment was strongest, embraced it and contributed with their own *haskalah*, a Jewish 'Enlightenment' movement. Secular learning was thought to be the answer to ostracization and an entry point to all areas of society. Traditionalists, though, opposed this move, fearing it would weaken Jewish learning, while European society still kept Jews at bay.

Political emancipation, which started after the French Revolution, proceeded rather painfully, underlined constantly by anti-Jewish feeling. Jewish reaction was varied. Intellectual factions believed that it was time to put aside all vestiges of 'primitive' superstition and were embarrassed by Jews from less enlightened areas who stuck to old ways based on prayer and traditional belief in the supernatural. In Russia, in particular, the large Jewish community was subject to the liberalizing and regressive swings of the ruling Tsar.

In Germany many Jews avidly joined in the new Reform movements where synagogue rituals were altered in line with modern demand, sometimes even taking place on Sunday instead of Saturday, the traditional Jewish Sabbath. Communities became increasingly outward-looking and eager for acceptability and took on board the new ideas on changing internal structures. In Russia and Poland, however, life continued very much as it had always done, even though nowhere was free of determined Enlighteners.

The backlash soon became evident. In Russia anti-Jewish activity progressed to new heights with both draconian legislation (such as enforced conscription and Russified education) and pogroms. In the West, from the 1870s, anti-Semitism became a movement.

From then on Jews began to resolve their own fate. In some traditional enclaves belief in the everlasting support of God continued as ever in the face of adversity. In others there was an increasingly intellectual and social approach. The drift away from traditional religious practice started in the *haskalah* turned the people instead to the ideology of nationhood and collective action, in some ways inspired by the ancient ideals of biblical Israel. Socialism – changing Jewish society where it was – and Zionism – turning away from Europe towards a Jewish homeland – were the new inspiration.

Meanwhile other sections of Jewish settlement were less troubled by such moves. Enterprising Jews were lured by the Americas and whole communities moved from Eastern Europe to make new lives in the new world. The Jews of India lived virtually untroubled lives for around 1,000 years, joined by Jews from the Middle East during the nineteenth century. In North Africa Jewish communities had a thriving life with their own traditions, while enduring secondary status and frequent hostility. The rich pattern of Jewish life in very

THE HOLOCAUST AND BEYOND

Jewish life in Europe reached intellectual and cultural heights during the first two decades of the twentieth century. The Enlightenment and emancipation movements had changed the face of society irretrievably. In the West Jews took a full part in the life around them and were open to stimulation from secular ideas. In Eastern Europe most Jews lived in severe poverty and the old ways of learning, piety and mysticism pertained.

All this was to be in ruins a quarter of a century later. The Holocaust has been much documented and the devastation to Jewish life mourned and remembered. Holocaust survivors for many years preferred not to talk about their experiences, trying to forget in the effort to regain normal lives. Only recently has there been a drive to help people come to terms with severe psychological pain by recounting their memories. The impetus not to forget has also led to the hounding of the perpetrators of war crimes and to demands for retribution.

There are many ways of coming to terms spiritually with the Holocaust. An obvious one is to turn to atheism, for if God existed, one has to ask why he allowed the atrocities to take place. Many Jews lost their faith after the Holocaust, yet there has also been a trend for those scarred by loss of home and family to reidentify with Judaism and even to return to traditional practice. However, this probably has more to do with the human need to know where you come from and where you belong than any more pronounced faith. The recommitment to Jewish identity, too, says much about renewed sensitivity to oppression and the determination never to let it happen again.

So where does this leave Judaism's faith in God, trust in the Divine will and commitment to a spiritual covenant? Most Jews get along perfectly well without answering any of these questions, yet still consider themselves perfectly paid-up members of the Jewish 'tribe'. Yet within the concentration camps and wartime ghettos the Jewish spirit did survive. Many survivors got by through relinquishing not only any form of spirituality but also of humanity, shutting off feeling in order to live from moment to moment. Others, though, kept up clandestine religious practices, finding their meaning in life by holding festival 'services', marking the start of the Sabbath and maintaining some semblance of the Passover Seder ritual.

To religious leaders the Holocaust is difficult – there seems no satisfactory explanation. Some attempts at explanation claim that it was a punishment for sin – Jews were becoming too assimilated and that this was God's way of bringing the people back to self-awareness. Equally hard to accept is the theory that the Holocaust was necessary in order to bring the state of Israel into existence, even if this holds some practical truth. Certainly there is a modern determination not to allow Hitler a posthumous victory – Jews must now become a strong identifiable force and not be absorbed to the point of extinction.

Often the resort is to the impossibility of knowing. God's ways, says Judaism, are impenetrable to man and we cannot ever really know where God was at that time and what his purpose was. Perhaps the answer most in line with the spirit of Judaism is to say that it is impertinent for us to expect that God will intervene in the ways of the world on our demand. The Holocaust denies the vision of God as a benign authority figure. God was then neither a loving father nor a wrathful avenger.

The fact of the Holocaust – like the destruction of the Temple, the Crusades, the Spanish Inquisition and the massacres and pogroms in Europe – is to an extent something we as the human race hold responsibility for. Like all catastrophes, personal or universal, much depends on how we survive. There are stories of Jews who marched praying and singing into the gas chambers, accepting the inevitability of death with their faith unimpaired and their hearts close to God. In the Jewish spiritual tradition, God was crying with his people and for the darkness of the human race. It was the spirit that remained defiant and faithful that also enabled God to survive.

ZIONIST IDEALS – ISRAELI REALITY

Zionism – the concept of a Jewish national homeland – arose as an amalgamation of traditional spiritual longing and modern political expediency. When the land of Israel had ceased to be the physical centre of Jewish life after AD 70 it became a centre for spiritual dreams. No matter what difficulties the Jewish people encountered in the Diaspora, return to the land of Israel was always bound up with the idea of redemption and restoration of their integrity as a people. Exile symbolized God's anger towards the Jews. Restoration implied their redemption.

The Israel they dreamed of was not a practical reality. Most Jews had little idea where it was, let alone what it was like. Zion was simply an idea, the embodiment of a time when Jews could live the idealized spiritual life without oppression. The powerful love of an idealized Holy Land was part and parcel of Jewish life.

The Messianic ideal was also incorporated into this concept. Return to Zion was seen as concurrent with the appearance of the Messiah. Thus it would have little to do with human effort, but would come about in God's own time. A minority of Jews in fact opposed the establishment of the state of Israel and still stand against it because of its formation through the insistence of man, not the word of God.

Back in nineteenth-century Europe the group consciousness of Jews as an exiled race yearning for a spiritual home had ceased to be a factor. The willing hunger for the Enlightenment and political emancipation had had a profound effect on Jewish thought. Jews no longer saw themselves as exiles in England, France and Germany but were eager to prove themselves loyal citizens. But even though assimilated, the Jewish people still held an attachment to Palestine, albeit historical and cultural, and there was financial support for resettlement into the rather unfriendly climate of a wasteland under Turkish rule. But rationalism made the Jewish people uncomfortable with basing life on spiritual concepts and Zion could no longer be held as a symbol of any future redemption.

The vast majority of Jews, however, were not emancipated in the nineteenth century and the real change of focus towards Zion came from the oppressed Russian Jewry. Where once the spiritual ideal had been bound up with religious fervour, in Russia the return to Zion became the practical answer to the overriding problem of anti-Jewish activity.

Elsewhere in Europe, emancipation was being accepted as a failure. Europeans seemed to tolerate Jews but would never completely accept them. Jewish thinkers thus began, from the late eighteenth century onwards, to voice their belief in a physical return to the homeland. They ranged from orthodox Rabbis advising the need for self-help to those desperate to get away from pogroms at all cost, while some still spoke up for the traditional spiritual relationship between Zion and the Jews.

The return movement accelerated during the early years of the twentieth century, with a new type of Jew eager for self-respect and self-determination. But modern Zionism proper only formed as a national movement with the arrival of Theodore Herzl, an assimilated journalist from Budapest who covered the anti-Semitically led trial of the Jewish army officer

Dreyfus in Paris. Herzl realized that the Jews urgently needed their own state for their physical and emotional survival. As political force joined up with Enlightenment disillusion, the flames of the old spiritual dream became fired. History, tradition, emotion and expediency ensured that the move towards the establishment of a homeland would become a relentless drive.

Throughout the early twentieth century, Jews fleeing persecution in Europe flooded into Palestine despite efforts by the British, responsible for the Mandate of Palestine after 1918, to keep a political status quo. Only after the extent of Second World War's destruction in Europe was revealed did it become possible for the state of Israel to be given its independence – to face an immediate Arab war.

So, although a cause for tremendous rejoicing, the establishment of the Israeli state was also heralded as the beginning of a bloodbath. The problems have hardly abated since. From a liberal humanitarian viewpoint, land has been taken unjustly from Arabs who had farmed it for centuries. From an emotional and historical viewpoint, the land is intimately bound up with the Jewish people and is now endemic to their national and religious survival. This dilemma was exacerbated after the Six Day War in 1967, when Israel gained embarrassingly large areas of land which have been disputed territory ever since. The counter-argument says that the land was justly won in a war in which Israel was not the aggressor and that Israel is justified in fearing for its security in the face of continuing threats from its neighbours.

Internally, too, Israel faces enormous struggles. It absorbs waves of immigrants from countries as different as Morocco and Russia. It has clashes between its largely secular population and growing religious fundamentalists. There are economic and social pressures of a fast-growing 'new-old' country. Still Israel has emotional and spiritual ties with the majority of Jews scattered throughout the world. Far from ideal, and a long way from heralding the Messianic Age, nevertheless the state is a source of hope and a symbol of survival.

It is also the birthplace of an entirely new Jewish spirit. The modern Israeli – part European, part Mediterranean, very Middle Eastern and largely Americanized – is far from the old-style Jew of Russia and Poland. Scratch the surface, though, and everything is there – Kabbalists steeped in traditions that go back to medieval Europe, Rabbis who can trace their learning back through illustrious ancestry, businesspeople as at home in the world as Spanish merchants, centres of study to rival those of Babylon. There is little in Israel that doesn't spark a deep chord in Jewish consciousness.

Where does the Jewish story go from here? Israel has become a fraught ideal, with many Jews pouring in from all corners of the world yet many more making the conscious decision that the Diaspora remains their home. Independence has brought its own problems. Whereas once Jews followed an unquestioning lifestyle, with obligations and customs no one would dream of disobeying, Judaism now requires hard choices. For the orthodox minority all over the world, life goes on as it always has done – in communities shielded from what is seen as an undesirable and an unappealing outside world. For the majority, though, Judaism is a matter of careful analysis and personal decision. How far and what to practise – synagogue membership, inner belief, alignment with Israel, community solidarity – these are all questions that thinking Jews have to face in the modern world.

SPIRITUALITY IN THE LIFE OF A JEWISH PERSON

S o far, we have looked at how the Jewish people held together and evolved as a community. We have seen how Jews adapted both to historical changes and to different cultures. We have traced how they fitted in yet remained apart, and how the dual forces of change and tradition enabled them to endure for 3,000 years.

This section looks at how Jews individually face the challenges involved in living a Jewish life. Life as a Jew is traditionally based around study (of the *Torah*, the first five books of the Bible), and observance of the commandments (*mitzvot*). These obligations are said to have been laid down by God and to be the bedrock of the consistent relationship with him. They occur first in the *Torah* itself and are expounded on at length in the *Talmud* and other works. The Rabbis eventually developed a carefully worked out scheme which interpreted God's direct rulings from the Bible itself and made them into a framework governing every aspect of life. This code of behaviour has been followed by every observant Jew ever since. It is not, however, a static set of rules. It is constantly evolving to include modern developments and needs.

The *mitzvot* fall into two groups – positive and negative – that is, those things you have to do and those you must refrain from.

66   Another definition, made by the Rabbis, is those obligations
between humans and God and those between individual people. There are 613 commandments in all. The 248 positive ones
have been linked with 248 body parts, showing us that they
cover all areas of human conduct. The 365 negative ones correspond to the days of the year, underlining the idea that they are
for all time. The positive commandments include praying at
appointed times, giving money to charity, keeping the festivals
and observing the dietary laws. Strict injunctions govern precisely how all these are to be done. The negative commandments include not speaking ill of anyone, not gossiping and not
eating unkosher animals.

The commandments may seem to be a set of rules and regulations. Spiritually, though, they are a way of keeping us in mind
of God and dealing properly with our fellow humans.

The *mitzvot* are subject to a variety of responses. A number of
them seem irrational, despite attempts by the greatest thinkers
to find ways of making them acceptable. The medieval philosophers in particular tried to find reasons both to satisfy questioning Jews and in order to display Judaism's rational basis.

Such ancient customs can certainly be eliminated by logic.
Today they are often dropped by people who intellectualize
them out of any meaning and purpose. They may also become
an empty habit, with perhaps the one positive virtue of helping
you keep in touch with the traditions of generations which
many modern Jews worry about breaking. But nothing says the
traditions should become mechanical rites. Jews are encouraged
to perform the *mitzvot* with the heart, with emotion and devotion. In this way, human desire and the intention to experience
life in a spiritual way imbue the commandments and the way of
life derived from them with meaning.

Also, today the non-rational is again an acceptable part of
religious faith. Judaism says that ultimately we cannot possibly

know God's ways. Trying to work them out with our paltry reasoning denies God's superior understanding. What matters is carrying out the *mitzvot*. That way we will have certain experiences and can reach our own understanding – not totally of God, but of the sacred.

Whether or not the commandments do have intrinsic Divine value is an open question. It is hard in this day and age to imagine God waiting with punishments for those who do not fulfil every one of his requirements. The question is not so much 'Does God really care?' as 'Do *we* care?' Without devotional intent, the commandments are empty rituals, meaningless to us and powerless for God.

PRAYER AND RITUAL

Those who argue that prayer is only binding by Rabbinic law have never seen the light. It is true that forms of the prayers are Rabbinic, and that prayers must be recited three times a day, but the concept of prayer and its essential idea belong to the very foundation of the *Torah*, namely, to know the Lord, to recognize His greatness and His glory with a serene mind and, through contemplation, to have these fixed firmly in the mind.

RABBI SHNEUR ZALMAN OF LIADY

Prayer is central to Jewish observance. The *Siddur*, the Jewish prayer book, is more widely circulated than the Bible. The word comes from 'order' – prayer needs to follow a certain order and itself imposes structure on Jewish life.

Prayer is most commonly undertaken together with the community, in a synagogue, but there are also prayers which are said in the home, for instance at the start of Sabbaths and festivals. If it is not possible to get together with a group of Jews to pray, the next best thing is to say the appointed prayer in private.

Some prayers, however, may only be said communally. The basic number of people required for a public service is 10 men – a *minyan*. This does not accord with current ideas of gender equality, but we will see later that women have traditionally their own separate prayer rituals and are not expected to meet the same requirements as men. A Jewish male is counted as a valid member of a prayer community after puberty – celebrated to coincide with his thirteenth birthday as his *bar-mitzvah*.

Prayer services are held three times a day – morning, afternoon and evening. One idea governing this ritual is that of the changing forces of nature – night into day according to the sun's movement. Prayer at the times of change brings God into focus as the power in charge of these perfectly normal yet also cosmic shifts. At Sabbaths and festivals extra prayers are added into the service.

One Hasidic leader said that he and his followers had souls not clocks – thus, they could only pray at their inner instigation, not just because the correct time had arrived. Ideally, this kind of soul prompting should be the true way to manage prayer.

Why do we pray at all? Prayer is part of human experience. Nowadays we can be rather ashamed to admit that we pray. Yet even people without religious affinity are moved at times to cry out to something in approximation to prayer, whether in joy, terror or misery. There seems to be a human need to contact something external to our own little universe, more so when life offers us abnormal experience. Alternatively, it is often impossible to pray, especially when we think we should. The atmosphere of a synagogue can be noisy and informal, and outsiders can feel shocked that services lack a sense of the sacred. Another bar is the nature of the prayer ritual. Traditionally carried out in Hebrew, it is a largely congregational matter which leaves you on the outside if you don't know either the language or the system. Many Jews have felt alienated and given up on prayer, even though retaining faith in their hearts.

Certainly it is best to have some sort of familiarity with the prayers. Many synagogues incorporate 'explanatory services' where the basic concepts underlying the prayers are related and discussed. A little understanding helps people participate without embarrassment and gives the prayers a more personal meaning. Then comes the true *kavannah* of prayer – its inner devotional motivation. This is Judaism's own form of meditation – the ritualistic prayers are a means of enabling you to access a frame of mind that can bring you into harmony with God's will.

Jewish prayer has four ostensible categories: petitioning God, thanking God, praising Him and confessing with soul-searching. The oldest forms of prayer, which go right back to pagan times, strongly emphasized supplication and worship. When everything seemed to depend on the vagaries of the gods it was natural to try to ingratiate yourself with the higher powers. The Jews transmuted this idea into a God of justice and mercy who would listen and help. Extolling God's virtues meanwhile became a way of concentrating on God's supremacy and 'otherness'.

The mystical imperative brought into play the sense of personal communication with God. Prayer could affect God as much as it changed the praying human. Prayer also had the effect – especially needed in a pre-psychoanalytical age – of offloading guilt and coming to terms with human error. Nowadays it represents all these things. A central shared feature which gives strength to the community, it connects the modern day to ancient time and ritual. It can also offer the psychological benefits of reaching out for help, countering loneliness, experiencing intimacy, finding connection and freeing emotional expression.

PRAYERS JEWS PRAY

In Judaism prayer is very much prescribed for you, although there is nothing to stop you praying in your own words. Yet the existing prayer is designed to encourage spiritual feeling, not mechanical repetition. Since it is hard to voice your own prayer without feeling self-conscious or inadequate, having something ready-made can link you into the right mood and attitude.

The *Shema* is the first prayer children are taught and is said both in synagogue and at home – traditionally when getting up in the morning and going to sleep at night. The *Shema* is a simple declaration of faith in God, reminding you to 'love the Lord your God with all your heart, and with all your soul and with all your might'. It is said in times of joy and also of despair, and it affirms the central belief of Judaism. The prayer is supposed to be said clearly aloud, with great inner concentration. The start of the *Shema* especially requires this state of mind and it is customary to close your eyes while reciting it. It is the only prayer which promises a specific reward for obeying God's commandments – that life will flow according to a gracious natural order.

The *Kaddish* prayer is perhaps the best known of all. Recited in memory of the dead, it is only said with a congregation of 10 and never privately. The prayer is actually nothing to do with death, but is a declaration of belief in God's holiness. It has many moods – it can be intoned mournfully and seriously, chanted emotionally yet also sung with great joy and optimism. It refers back to the prophetic vision of Ezekiel, who saw a time when God's greatness would be celebrated by all people, and it expresses deep longing for the God's kingdom to be established on Earth.

Shmonei Esrei, the Eighteen Blessings, forms the centre of every service and is said morning, noon and night. It is also known as the *Amidah*, 'Standing', since the prayer is said standing up to be fully in awe of God. It has different versions for weekdays, Sabbaths and festivals. The *Amidah* is said facing towards Jerusalem, and in Jerusalem, facing towards the site of the Temple. Feet should be together, copying the stance of the

angels in Ezekiel 1. The prayer is said as an almost silent meditation, with the lips moving but the voice not heard, and in deep inner concentration. It is a mixture of praising God and petitioning him to meet our needs and thanks. On the Sabbath and festivals the prayer is shortened to focus on the sanctity of the day rather than on any lack of fulfilment, since it is forbidden to dwell on personal need. It is customary to bend the knees and bow to God during the blessings. The prayer is a reminder of God's powers in both everyday life – sustaining and healing – and in cosmic terms: he can create from nothing and also recreate from the dead. An act of intense reverence, the *Amidah* is a way of connecting God's highest powers with our deepest hopes for ourselves.

The public reading of the *Torah*, passage by passage through the first five books of the Bible from week to week, is not a prayer in itself but a prayerful act – learning the word of God, and therefore a form of divine worship. The portion is read three times each week – Monday, Thursday and on Saturday. The first two were market days in the ancient world and thus an ideal time to get people congregated together to listen and study.

The scrolls are taken from the Ark of the synagogue and the appropriate part is traditionally read in Hebrew incantation. It is followed by a reading from the Prophets. The scrolls are then processed around the synagogue before being returned to the Ark. The reverence given to the scrolls and the chanting surrounding the reading help to implant the words themselves in the mind of those who listen. The procession ritual has ancient echoes and the scrolls – the *Torah* handwritten on parchment – are time-honoured Judaic symbols. The reader reads on behalf of all the community, and various people 'called up' to the *Torah* recite blessings over each section of the whole portion, an honour recalling the first meeting with the word of God at Sinai.

Modern prayer evolved out of biblical sacrifice. When Abraham turned away from the worship of idols and conceived of one God, worship began to embrace other elements apart from sacrifice to appease a chosen deity. Even while sacrifices (now confined to animal rather than the human of pagan tradition) were still central, i.e. as long as the Jerusalem Temple was still standing, prayer supplemented the rite and was largely free and spontaneous. It brought a personal, confessional aspect into the earlier forms of petition and praise.

It was only in the Second Temple period after 485 BC that the daily prayers became more fixed. The Psalms and the Book of Daniel both mention the thrice daily prayer ritual. Sacrificial offerings were made three times a day and the scribe Ezra, who was trying to introduce stricter religious order, deliberately made them correspond. There was an extra offering on Sabbaths and holidays and so an additional prayer has also been incorporated for those times. The Israelites had to be assured after the destruction of the Temple that their prayers were just as effective as sacrifice in reaching God. Their timing gave them replacement status and put people spiritually in touch with what had gone before.

Well before the destruction of the Temple synagogues existed as the home of informal prayer assemblies. They could have come into being at the time of the Babylonian exile, in the sixth century BC, or even earlier. Each area had its prayer gathering and representatives went to Jerusalem to take part in the Temple sacrifice in turn. Their community would pray at the same time as their delegation was observing the ritual in Jerusalem.

One of the oldest known prayers is the *Shema*, which, as already mentioned, has a central place in the ritual today. Its recital is mentioned in the Bible as a twice daily duty. Also very

old is the Blessing of the Priests. This was an important part of the Temple services. The priests, *kohanim*, who received the blessing were instruments through which God's blessing came to the people. The *Kaddish* prayer, which exists in different versions, also goes back to the Second Temple period. Knowing that what you are saying was also said by Jews 1,000 or more years ago creates a sense of continuity and of forging links in a long chain.

Prayers were originally learned by heart – none were written down until around the eighth century AD, when the first prayer books came into use. The prayer book used today comes from the ninth century AD.

The prayers as we know them were mostly composed during the Rabbinic period (first to sixth century AD) but they were based on more ancient formulations. Chanting and melody have also been used since ancient times and the *Talmud* says a pleasant voice is necessary for a prayer leader.

Mysticism is represented strongly in prayer, though most people do not recognize its links with the liturgy. The repetition, for instance, echoes mystical chanting, in which the words were not meant to make sense but to induce a state of mind wholly concentrated on God. The *sefirot* – aspects of God – have also crept into the liturgy. There are many references to God's majesty, beauty, power and victory, noticeably when the scrolls are processed to the Ark. Another much-loved system of the mystics – describing God in terms of the human body – is also in evidence, especially in the Hymn of Glory often sung at the end of services. Since it was not permitted to create an artistic image of God (which was dangerously close to idol worship), these verbal descriptions assisted knowledge and visualization of a form you could engage with.

Prayer does not always remain static. Changes and additions have kept it alive over the years. In a move to make the prayers more relevant to modern times, the Reform movement has done away with much of repetition. The Reform prayer book introduces new prayers relating to the Holocaust and modern concerns, and has meditation passages from modern sources. It has also changed the order of service and uses a freer English translation to get rid of anachronisms.

IN PRIVATE AND IN COMMUNITY

As part of a community prayer helps to strengthen ties with an extended 'family' and gives a sense of place. Sometimes it seems that going to the synagogue is almost like being part of a club, but it has a positive function in providing a sense of belonging.

Communal worship fills many needs. Prayers recited as a community stress the plural, and thus the oneness of the people as a whole. The act of praying together multiplies a prayer's spiritual power – as with any public gathering, the energetic force is more concentrated. Communal worship also enables the sharing of private occasions such as birth, after which special baby blessings are said, and death, after which the *Kaddish* prayer is recited together with all the community.

Though it may seem as if only those 'in the know' feel comfortable in community worship, actually synagogue ritual grew up to guard the unscholarly from embarrassment. The Rabbi or prayer leader (who does not have to be Rabbinically learned) recites the liturgy for everyone, so it is not strictly necessary to know the prayers at all.

Many prayers are said privately too. Morning, afternoon and evening prayer is often recited alone if one is unable to get to a synagogue. Adult males (over the *bar-mitzvah* age of 13) are supposed to put on *tefillin* at weekday morning services, either at home or in the synagogue. These consist of two boxes

containing sections of the *Torah* (including the *Shema*) on parchment and leather straps which bind them to the body, to the weaker of the two arms (the left if you are right-handed) and the head. This is done in the spirit of 'binding' the word of God physically to you (the injunction is stated in Exodus and Deuteronomy), remembering that God is opposite the heart, and so subjecting its longings to his service, and upon the head, so the mind and brain can be constantly influenced by him.

Other important home prayer rituals take place at the lighting of the Sabbath candles. This is a female responsibility unless there is no woman present. The blessing is a simple one, reminding us that it is God's commandment to light the Sabbath lights. Additional blessings are said at home before eating bread, over wine and at the end of the Sabbath. There are blessings for putting on new clothes, using something for the first time, going on a journey and successfully completing it, eating the first fruits of the season and even getting up and going to sleep. All of this helps to keep God in mind as the Creator of all things and remind us that we are not in sole charge of our world.

WOMEN AND PRAYER

Women are often said to be left out of the Jewish prayer ritual. They do not have the same obligations to pray as men and do not count as part of the *minyan* required for communal prayers. Modern dilemmas have been caused by the thanksgiving said in one of the daily prayers that God 'has not made me a woman'. This may not, however, be as degrading as it seems – it may refer to a special spiritual experience for which a man would naturally express his gratitude. As women are exempt from praying at fixed times, so men have more opportunities to fulfil the *mitzvot*, and in the context of Rabbinic times, when

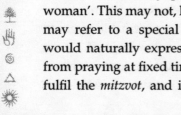

prayer was consolidated, the more you could do religiously the better, because you would thereby become close to God. (In fact many orthodox women observe the thrice daily prayer ritual in their own homes and own time as a matter of choice.) Also possible is that men were giving thanks for avoiding the suffering of women in childbirth.

Many leading Rabbinic scholars do in fact perceive the position of women in Judaism as being superior to that of men. It is for this reason that women do not need the same dedication to prayer as men. The Hebrew word for womb, *rehem*, has the same root as the word for compassion, thus a woman is equated with this aspect and needs less spiritual refining than a man. Supporting this view is the fact that in the story of Creation, woman followed man in an ascending order of superiority of the species – and was the completing factor in the universe.

In the traditional synagogue service, women are not allowed to take part in the *Torah* reading, although in Reform and Liberal communities they have equal status. Traditionally, the voice of a woman in song (as in the chanting of a prayer) is not supposed to be heard by a group of men. A positive interpretation of this is that the beauty and divinity of a woman in prayer could too easily distract the men from their devotions!

In traditional congregations where women choose to observe segregation from men in prayer, they sit separately and may have their own separate *Torah* service where they read from the scroll and pass it around to be handled as do the men. Women who prefer this tradition say that the opportunity to pray within an all-female group is empowering in itself. The dynamic created by a mixed gathering is different from that of single-sex groups and praying separately can focus your attention. Sitting amongst other women also has an advantage in the modern world of split families. Separated or single women need not feel

78   awkward because they are not with a male partner, but are equal among other women.

Orthodoxy defends traditional patterns as providing recognition of the spiritual differences between men and women. Such explanations often fall short for those embarrassed by what seem like male-dominated rituals and hidebound inequalities. But modern Judaism has a place for those who demand full integration as well as those satisfied with the traditions.

DUTY AND PLEASURE

Prayer is an obligation, yet it is not supposed to become a chore. Like any commitment, it has both requirements and rewards. It began as something taken on willingly in order to keep us linked to God. Nowadays we have a more ambivalent relationship to it. How does the Jew ensure that praying is not an empty ritual? The mechanical mumbling of ancient passages has put many modern Jews off the whole concept of prayer and synagogue-going may seem a farcical irrelevance. Now committed Jews are aiming to create their own relationship to prayer so they can keep it fresh and meaningful.

One way of looking at prayer is to see it as necessary for God. It is said that God longs for the prayers of the righteous, that he is in need of our prayers as a way of knowing we still require his presence amongst us. Thus we pray not just so we can get what we want or because of a historical injunction to do so, but to ensure that we are people of God and are close to God.

Prayer also has an ethical dimension. We think we know how to behave and what to do, yet the ancient prayers act as a reminder of how to think and act. We ask God to help us in telling the truth and making us strong enough to bear ill-feeling against us. We acknowledge that we are human and therefore get things wrong, yet we always have the chance to see our faults and start anew. We recognize that we fall back yet always have somewhere to go, with our own self-will and the help of God. We see that it is ill-advised to put our faith in fallible humans, that only God's ways are worthwhile. We remember that there is a world of God that we constantly aspire to and a world of human nature which we can constantly purify.

The external demand to pray therefore must be fuelled from within, from the understanding of why we are praying. It has always been important in Judaism to pray with *kavannah*, a mixture of concentrated intention and devotion. When Jewish thought became too taken up with philosophy and rationalism, there was always the cry to come back to the heart, to faith and inner feeling. From the Middle Ages, the 'duties of the heart', the inner meaning of prayer, have been emphasized. The Hasidic movement brought this to a head with its extreme contemplation on prayer, turning prayer into meditative ritual in which each sound was chanted to allow it to permeate and transform the whole being. The Hasidim often took huge amounts of time just in the preparatory rituals before prayer in order to bring themselves to the right state of mind in which to approach the holy words. We can do this in part today. While praying as part of a commitment is important, the attitude with which we pray is equally meaningful.

What language should a Jew use for prayer? Hebrew, the traditional language of Jewish prayer, can be a problem if it is unfamiliar. More important is to pray in a language you relate to, to understand what you are saying. It is useful to find a translation of the prayers which you find personally evocative – too many are archaic and uninspiring. It also helps when in a synagogue not to leave the praying to those who seem to know what to do. Praying, private or public, is not really a spectator sport. Involving your heart and mind as far as possible is an essential step.

PRINCIPLES OF JEWISH SPIRITUALITY

THE UNANSWERED PRAYER

What do you do when prayers don't come true?

One traditional story tells of a traveller in Heaven. He sees a store of parcels stacked up, each one stamped and addressed and ready to send out. He asks, 'Why are those parcels waiting there?' The reply: 'They are the answers to people's prayers, but just as they were about to be sent the people gave up and stopped asking, so the connection was lost and the parcel is unable to find its recipient.' We are told – never lose hope!

There are plenty of stories of people who carried on praying in steadfast faith and whose prayers were miraculously answered. An infertile woman prays at the *kotel*, the Western Wall said to be the remnant of the Jerusalem Temple, a potent place for prayer. After years of trying, she finally conceives. An 'incurable' cancer suddenly goes into remission, helped by communal prayer. Prayer can work for the best.

Harder to come to terms with is when we pray and the worst still happens. A soldier is captured and his picture shown on television, crying and pleading for mercy. (This happened in Israel in 1994.) The whole country prays for his release. He is shot dead. The response from his mother: 'Sometimes God says no.' Shortly afterwards his family founded a centre for peace between Arabs, by whom her son was captured, and Israelis.

Sometimes it seems there is nothing we can do to get God to listen. Children die, the pious suffer, bad people live, Genocide happens. Prayers are not always answered. Logic may conclude that God does not exist, but the spiritual answer is not to become bitter or disillusioned. The Baal Shem Tov, the Hasidic master, held that prayer is always answered, but often in a way which is hidden from us. If you wait for your prayers to be answered, he said, you introduce the corporeal to your prayers. The answer may not be what you expect, or what you want, or indeed anything to do with you personally at all.

Disappointment in prayer may simply result from imbuing it with high expectation. We want God to meet our needs, but we do not seek to find out what are His. Accepting that our will is not always God's will is also part of the greater picture of prayer.

BIRTH AND DEATH

A man arrived at the gates of the World to Come apologizing
profusely for not having lived his life as well as a famous sage.
He was asked, 'But did you live your life as well as *you* could
have done?'

HASIDIC STORY

What does Judaism say about the age-old riddle, the
purpose of life? Time and again the teachings stress
that we are not here solely to have all the pleasure we
can get. If this were so, there would be no explanation for
human suffering and inequality. We are simply assigned this
lifetime to achieve whatever potential we have, according to
the talents and opportunities we have been given. This life is a
place through which we pass on our way to the world after
death. It is how we live now, enduring hardships, appreciating
gifts and helping our fellow beings, that will determine our
spiritual life when we leave the present body behind.

There is no separation in biblical thought between the body
and the soul. Only when it came to the Rabbinic period did the
dual concept come in. The human body was thought to belong
to the material world and the soul to come from Heaven – a
mixture therefore of animal and angel. The two, however, had

to co-exist in a spiritual way, with the body kept fit to house the soul. This idea has persisted to the present day.

The concept of the soul became more complex during the medieval period, when it was divided into the three categories of *nefesh*, *ruah* and *neshamah*. The Kabbalists expanded on this still further, defining *nefesh* as the basic soul force, the *ruah* as the higher inspiration (its translation is 'breath') that makes us transcend everyday reality and the *neshamah* as a high state of spiritual development only brought about through God. The whole of the soul was considered to interact between Heaven and Earth and could inhabit both realms.

A NEW JEWISH SOUL

Bringing forth a new Jewish soul is intrinsic to Judaism, which is known for its emphasis on family life. Having children is considered a special blessing. Why are we so delighted when we see a young child? One Jewish answer is that the baby is still very close to its conception and carries with it some of the ecstasy of that time.

Contraception is not exactly outlawed in Judaism, but it would be highly unlikely for a traditional Jewish couple to decide against children. Procreation is considered a *mitzvah*, a commandment in its own right in accordance with the biblical commandment in Genesis 1 to be fruitful and multiply. Orthodox families do not artificially prevent conception, believing that each child is a gift from God – so long as it is possible to have children, you should do so. Contraception is generally a matter for individual couples to decide on according to the strictness of their interpretation of the law and their own circumstances.

Childlessness is of course experienced by Jewish couples as a result of infertility. In such cases, treatment is encouraged and

in Israel fertility treatment is widely available and free of charge. Adoption is another course. Children do not necessarily have to be Jewish at birth but those who are not are converted and then brought up as Jewish.

A baby's birth is a cause for rejoicing not just on a personal level but because each child enriches the family of Judaism. When a baby is born mystical tradition says that an angel lays its finger over its lips (thereby creating the cleft above the upper lip), and in that instant the soul forgets all previous existence and must begin as if anew. Thus the education of a child in Jewish values is the obligation of Jewish parents.

INITIATION TO JUDAISM – THE RITE OF CIRCUMCISION

A male child's first initiation to Judaism is the rite of circumcision. The operation is usually carried out on the eighth day after birth. While traditional Jews hold the ceremony at home, others can conform to tradition in hospital under the guise of a sensible medical decision. Circumcision is so important that nothing, not even Shabbat or festivals on which daily life normally stops, can interfere. It is performed whatever day it is. Only if you have had two previous children die due to circumcision is the baby exempt.

Circumcision is a multi-faceted issue. On one hand it is an ancient rite of passage. The tradition has certainly been passed on virtually unchanged among Jews since biblical times and is the one least likely to be abandoned by Jews today. Rational thinkers, though, cannot fail to raise questions – is the whole procedure simply a remnant of ancient barbarism?

In Hebrew circumcision is *brit* – covenant. It signifies the covenant between Abraham and God. It is first referred to in Genesis 17, where as a sign of his promise to the one God Abraham

circumcised himself and the other men of his household. Now as
then, circumcision is quite simply an initiation rite into Judaism.

Many attempts have been made to explain the necessity for the
practice over and above this archaic factor. One says that the foreskin has no useful function and its removal makes the male closer
to perfection. (Presumably women are free of this inbuilt flaw.)
The drive to wrongdoing – first manifested by Adam's sin in the
Garden of Eden – is something we must all seek to avert.

Kabbalah, which applies the structure of the *sefirot* (aspects of
God) to everything, explains this in more detail. The penis is
represented by *yesod*, the foundation, the seat of creative power.
One function of this organ is clearly procreation. Contained
within creation, according to *Kabbalah*, is also destruction,
allowed by God in order for us to make a free choice. In this
case, the penis also discharges waste matter. Before Adam's sin,
the two functions – procreation and elimination – were separate
in him. Once he sinned, the two channels became one. His penis
was covered by the foreskin, from which the evil urge derived
its sustenance. If Adam hadn't sinned, the world would have
reached perfection, with nothing going to waste. So the foreskin
served as a reminder of both the 'waste' that is in man and of
the destructive force contained in the sexual urge. Removing it
can thus divert the sexual impulse to holiness.

The fact that we ourselves have to perform the operation
shows us how to be partners with God in creating perfection in
the universe. The removal of the foreskin suggests we should
not assume that all is in order in the 'natural' world. There are
occasions when we can improve on nature in a way that transforms and transcends it.

Such mystical interpretations became mythologized into a
popular perception of the foreskin being 'unclean'. This can,
however, be a valid interpretation in the physical realm. Nowadays for 'unclean' we may simply read 'unhygienic', hence the

foreskin is routinely removed in many secular cultures – circumcision is a standard procedure in America, for example. This argument has enabled circumcision to be carried out unquestioned in the modern world, with logic to justify it.

The debate about circumcision continues as many Jews wonder about its viability in the modern world. Yet in the end the decision is already made. In the chain of tradition circumcision is so essential that few Jews feel they have the right to choose against it.

THE REDEEMED FIRSTBORN

The firstborn male child (except a Cohen or Levy, descendants of the ancient priests) is also required to go through the ceremony of Redemption of the Firstborn (*pidyon ha-ben*), which takes place 31 days after birth.

The ceremony comes from a commandment in the Book of Numbers 18 and has been established for certain from around AD 200. Money is paid symbolically to a Cohen, in memory of the ancient priestly tribe, and is passed over the child as the price of redemption. The money is then usually given to charity.

The concept behind the ceremony is that the firstborn has a particular form of holiness and should be fit to become a priest. Since the *kohanim* became the priestly caste (anyone with the surname 'Cohen' is said to be a descendant of this caste), the payment made is in lieu of the child joining the priesthood. Another possible explanation is to do with the Exodus from Egypt, prior to which the Pharaoh ordered the killing of every firstborn male – thus the offering is in thanksgiving for this redemption.

The rite is not so widely carried out as circumcision – Reform Judaism has largely given up the custom, while other branches of Judaism are introducing similar ceremonies for daughters.

Again, however, it represents a link in the chain of tradition and is taken as a special thanksgiving for the first son. It is also a way of dedicating the family to God from its inception.

THE GIVING OF NAMES

When a baby is born it is customary to give it a Hebrew name in addition to its English name. Baby girls are named in synagogue shortly after birth, boys are named at their circumcision ceremony. The Hebrew name is used at all religious ceremonies, most importantly at marriage and death.

The Hebrew name is said to be the name that carries on after death and is remembered at the time of resurrection, when the souls of the dead, it is said, will be reclothed in human bodies.

Repeating daily a biblical verse which begins with the first letter and ends with the last letter of the person's Hebrew name is a way of ensuring that it is kept alive. Names are usually biblical, with the *Ashkenazi* custom being to call the child after a dead relative, while the *Sephardim* may honour the living.

Traditionally the name of a sick person may be changed so that any evil which has become attached to the old name can be released and better fortune ensue.

The principles of *gematria*, a Hebrew form of numerology, can also be employed when it comes to naming or choosing a new name. Words can be linked according to their numerical value, creating associations of ideas. Thus, consciously choosing a certain name can tie you to a positive concept.

Taking on a Hebrew name, or using yours in preference to that on your birth certificate, often accompanies the desire to identify with your Jewish side. People returning to Judaism or becoming more observant (or going to live in Israel where Hebrew names are familiar) often become known by their Hebrew name.

NOT THE END – THE JEWISH VIEW OF DEATH

In Judaism death is not the end, but the beginning of the soul's entry to the World to Come. It is accompanied by strict ritual procedures. Having a set procedure helps make order out of what can be a period of emotional chaos.

Death is said to be a time when two worlds kiss. The soul is said to part company with the body and to return to the place it came from. This process of departure is gradual and may begin as early as 30 days before the actual time of death. It takes approximately a year for the soul to detach fully from the body and during this time it lives in an in-between stage where it may have some contact with the living world. The peacefulness of this transition is governed by the kind of life the person lived in this world and also by the prayers of those left behind.

Is the World to Come the place where the individual soul gains immortality or is it the resurrection (prophesied by Ezekiel's vision of the valley of dry bones), when the dead come back to life from the grave? In medieval times the Rabbis held great debates on which was correct. Nowadays the traditional view is that both are true. The whole picture is, however, dependent on the arrival of the Messiah. When that happens the souls which are resting in an immortal state will re-enter the resurrected bodies.

The process can be looked at, less fancifully, as the beginning of a better world. When the world is set to rights, with ourselves as the chief movers in this process, then there is hope that souls will be reunited and the human race become whole. So, the World to Come, though associated with a vague and distant Messianic Age, can still be regarded as an immediate possibility which our present-day actions are helping bring about. It is a time when spiritual joy will exist for all human beings. Other expressions for the World to Come are the Hereafter or the Garden of Eden, but not Heaven.

What happens to the wicked? Hell is not a strong factor in Judaism. The souls of the wicked simply find God unreachable even after dying. The most wicked of all are said to die with the body and thus have no chance of eternal bliss.

A type of hell known as *gehinom* is reserved for souls which need punishment. This is more of a cleansing and curing process than a true punishment. Jewish teaching sees the process in terms of someone who is ill and needs to be treated. Sometimes the treatment is painful and unpleasant, like having a tooth extracted or undergoing chemotherapy. Such is the pain of extricating the 'bad' from the soul – it can be long and difficult and the soul suffers much in the process but may eventually be healed and return to life. Life itself here on Earth can have the same effect if a person has to undergo much suffering during it. Life can feel like a punishing experience, but it is possible to work with suffering and 'alchemize' oneself so that the good, healthy, humane parts become strong.

Traditional teachings do not say much about the journey of the soul after the death of the body, although Kabbalists have said much more on the whole subject. They believe strongly in reincarnation, that the soul can return to Earth in another body. Great Kabbalists like Isaac Luria of Safed were clairvoyant enough to be able to look at a person and read what kind of previous lives they had been through and what their present existence was for. The Jewish view of reincarnation differs from that of the Eastern religions in that it makes no reference to present suffering reflecting past personal wrongdoing – it is more the result of the sins of previous generations. The ability to deal with suffering in this lifetime is to do with strengthening faith in God's will.

If Judaism believes that life continues after death, why is there not more emphasis on this afterlife? Traditionally Jews

have been advised to steer clear of this area because it can raise all sorts of possibilities of false hope and expectation. What happens after death cannot really be known and attempting to find out can lead to spurious conclusions. The magical practices associated with contacting the dead were also used by pagan cults and Judaism sought to disassociate itself from them. Even though this world is strongly regarded as the gateway to the World to Come, speculating on the afterlife is not as useful as concentrating on what we can do here and now. Recognizing this 'gateway' stage is full of imperfections, Judaism still encourages you to be totally here, doing your best, rather than escaping into speculative fantasy. Living in a way that constantly helps to improve the everyday world is the best preparation for the life to come.

ATTENDING THE DEAD

It is considered a great privilege to perform the sacred duty of attending a dead body. It is both a last respect to the person who has died and a way of giving to the family, who may be too emotionally distraught to perform the intricacies of the carefully prescribed ritual themselves.

Burials take place as soon as possible after death, and watchers look after the corpse and prepare it for the ceremony. This phase is when the corpse is supposed to be particularly vulnerable – physically from deterioration and psychically while the soul reaches for the Hereafter. While 'watching', psalms are recited. This originated in the belief that the soul must be accompanied by the sacred while it detaches from the physical.

The preparation of the body, which includes combing the hair and cleaning the nails, includes a set of purification rituals performed with respect and reverence. Many of the rituals' details are kabbalistic in origin. Using egg in washing the head is one.

According to seventeenth-century Kabbalists, the egg signifies the process of death and rebirth. The body should be kept covered as much as possible, even while being washed, to avoid any disrespect. Warm water is used and the whole washing ceremony is a ritual portrayal of the ceremony of *mikveh* – purification in water – which Jews perform at key points during life. Washing is performed in a precise order, with the head – the most important area and that which emerges first into the world – cleansed first. Nothing must be passed across the body, allowing space, both physical and etheric, between the living and the dead, for the protection of both, and to ensure free passage toward Heaven for the soul.

Prayers are recited, asking for mercy for the dead person and that they may be allowed to rest with righteous souls. Corpses are dressed in a simple shroud, a custom set down by the Rabbis in order not to shame those who couldn't afford elaborate costumes for their dead. Men are wrapped in their *tallit* (prayer shawl).

No remuneration is received for attending the dead. It allows for all to be treated equally and for true care to be given to both the dead and the living.

JEWISH BURIAL

The Hebrew word for burial is *levayyah* and it means 'to accompany' the dead to their resting-place. Attending a funeral is another *mitzvah*, a special deed of respect and kindness. The early Rabbis taught that no corpse should be left unburied overnight, but today most Jews are buried the day after they die. Cremation is not usual, although Reform Jews do sometimes now cremate their dead. Cremation is considered a sudden and unnatural destruction of the living form which may interfere with both the soul's departure and the possibility of its

eventual resurrection. Apart from this, cremation was originally seen as a pagan custom and is now repugnant due to its association with the gas chambers of the Holocaust.

The coffins used at a Jewish burial are simple wooden ones. In Israel no coffin is used at all – the corpse is buried directly in the earth, to be as close as possible to the holy soil.

The custom of 'rending the garments', carried out either on hearing of the death of someone in the immediate family or just before their funeral, is referred to in the Bible. A small cut or tear may be made to a garment worn over or close to the heart, as a sign of grief – for parents, on the left side, closest the heart, and for other relatives at the right. A small scarf can be used. The tear echoes and intensifies the sense that things are no longer whole, that something has been destroyed. The torn garment is supposed to be mended later – crookedly for a parent, straight for others – and this can be part of the process of healing the emotional wound.

Jewish burials can seem rather stark to the outsider. Flowers and wreaths are not used at funerals – probably, again, to disassociate from non-Jewish customs. Instead, stones are laid on the grave. One reason for this is the Talmudic belief, embellished by mysticism and superstition, that souls may still live in the grave with the body for a time and should be helped to stay down so they can depart slowly and not interfere with the living. Stones also provide a sense of solidity and of building a wall between life and death.

A short service referring to the life of the deceased precedes the procession to the grave. Seven pauses are made during the procession, recalling the seven vanities mentioned in the Book of Ecclesiastes. After the coffin has been lowered, each person, in order of closeness to the deceased, throws earth on top of it. In this way, each mourner can make final contact with the deceased and feel a personal contribution to the burial ceremony.

On leaving the cemetery you are required to wash your hands
– both to rid yourself of contact with death and as a symbol of
permitting yourself to carry on with the 'running water' of life.

GRIEF EXPRESSED – THE JEWISH WAY OF MOURNING

Immediately after the funeral comes the period of mourning.
Many rituals attend this time. It starts with the *shivah*, seven
days of mourning for close relatives (father, mother, son, daugh-
ter, brother, sister, husband, wife). The *shloshim* is the period
lasting 30 days after the funeral, during which restrictions
apply to the mourners. After this, for the next 11 months those
mourning their parents continue to observe certain rituals and
must say the *Kaddish* prayer daily with a congregation.

The *shivah* is a time of withdrawal from the world and normal
activity. For this reason, some find it abnormally restrictive and
distressing – non-orthodox Jews usually only observe a day
or two of mourning. The seven-day mourning period is said to
correspond to the seven days in which the world was made,
thus representing the whole cycle of creation.

Many find taking this time off can be a great relief – a permissible way of exploring and expressing grief. Friends and family
visit the house of mourning, where the mourners sit on low
chairs, reflecting their emotional state. Mourners do not work or
take part in any social events. They do not attend to normal
household affairs and visitors are supposed to bring food so
they do not have to cook. The idea is that the mourner is a kind
of guest, cared for in their own home, with no distractions from
the process of mourning. Visitors greet the mourner first, thus
removing even social obligations from them. For the rest of
the month mourners do not go to social gatherings or places
of entertainment.

The first meal after the funeral is supposed to include life-affirming foods, such as egg and bread. A candle is kept alight for the whole of the seven days in memory of the dead person and signifying the light of their soul. During the *shivah* it is customary to cover all mirrors, perhaps because they give us occasion to reflect on ourselves while this is a time for dwelling on and with the deceased. There is a suggestion here, too, of the separation between our real selves and our reflected selves, or the self of life and of death, which are already dangerously intermingled at the time of death. So care is taken to reaffirm their different realms.

The mourning period, although restricting, is not necessarily a time of unmitigated misery. It is a time when the deceased is talked about and remembered, often with affection and humour. The Jewish mourning ritual is now thought to be highly valuable therapeutically. It gives social support and reaffirms the continuity of friendships and family life. It gives permission to grieve and relief from all pretence at carrying on stoically. It allows you to face emotional trauma honestly and offers time and space in which to come to terms with the reality of death.

Yet Jewish law also admonishes against excessive grief. For this reason, after the seventh day the mourner is expected to 'get up' – figuratively and emotionally – and get on with life. Grief is given full rein in the Jewish tradition. But life takes precedence.

RELATIONSHIP
AND INTIMACY

One who does not marry dwells without blessing, without goodness, without peace.

THE TALMUD

S
ince Jewish life is traditionally based around the family, it
is no wonder that Judaism has a lot to say about male/
female relationship. There is a kind of dual thread running
through the Jewish approach. On one hand, Judaism has been
associated with a liberal attitude – certainly in comparison with
Christianity's moral stance and the guilt it has traditionally
inspired. From what appears as the outpouring of love in certain biblical passages (the Song of Songs the most explicit) to the
joyous celebration of life of the Hasidic sects, the inference has
been that Judaism favours enjoyment of love and sex.

This is not necessarily the case. Also at play is a strong ascetic
attitude. The more extreme forms of Judaism such as the pietis-
tic sects *(see pp. 43 and 48)* viewed relationships between the
sexes with extreme caution. Although people were supposed to
marry, those with spiritual aspirations saw the relationship
between man and woman as a pale reflection of the glory of
the relationship between man and God. Literature suggests that
human intimacy is often a troublesome area and there are

warnings against taking pleasure in it for its own sake. It should be regarded strictly as accentuating the possibilities for unifying the Divine structure.

Ambivalent attitudes resulting from a clash between earthly desire and heavenly aspiration certainly occupied the Jews of the Middle Ages and the early modern period. Love and sexual union were often written about, sometimes very graphically. But this can be considered a metaphor for religious ecstasy rather than the endorsement of unbridled intimacy. Today Judaism tends to steer a middle path, focusing on the desirability of a committed relationship.

The early Rabbis paid attention to the practicalities of relationship and gave detailed advice on how intimacy was best conducted. Much of their thinking has come down to us today in conservative attitudes and families are very much involved in overseeing suitable liaisons. Ultra-orthodox Jews still tend to 'arrange' marriages – not actually such a shocking anachronism, since in practice the system works not dissimilarly from a dating agency and with more chance of compatible choices. Both parties meet several times and have the freedom to accept or reject one another. In Israel there is an open emphasis – sometimes surprising in such a modern society – on the desirability of finding your partner and on the whole structure of family life.

Homosexual relationships are not tolerated within traditional Judaism, which bases its stance on the biblical prohibition. Probably this originated from the need to propagate the species and the fact that homosexual relationships would deny women family status and children. There is less stringency against lesbian relationships, although they are also outlawed in traditional circles.

Spiritually, the nature of relationship in Judaism is seen as reflecting that between humankind and God. It also holds perhaps the highest possibility – more so than any other human activity – of establishing harmony between the *sefirot*, the various streams of Divine energy at play in the world. This is why Judaism has attempted to understand it in human terms while creating restrictions to prevent it becoming debased.

In emphasizing the importance of relationship, Judaism has parted company somewhat with modern attitudes. Nowadays independence is seen as highly desirable. The differences between men and women are stressed and their often irreconcilable approaches blamed for relationship breakdowns. Modern society encourages attempts at 'understanding', but at the same time people are expected to function as single units. Judaism, however, takes a view with its roots in a different era and its expectations in another reality – though conversely, it is one which touches the heart of our most romantic dreams. This vision sees man and woman as part of a spiritual whole. Separately, each is a lesser being, missing an essential component for life.

A way of interpreting the story of Creation favoured by mystics corroborates this view. It sees Adam as originally an androgynous being. When God created woman, he caused a split which also made Adam into a male. Adam's sin, which exacerbated this division, provided further potential for catastrophe – which can be averted by correct human action to reunify the two sides.

Jewish teachings submit that men and women function better together and should do everything they can to ensure they meet the right partner and build together as one. Judaism also strongly reinforces an idea that might be thought the product of New Age romance – that each soul has its true partner, a soulmate

who is carved from the same Divine material as itself. No romantic dream, this idea is part of Judaism's traditional writings, which say that this destiny is fixed 40 days after conception, at which point one's 'intended' is picked on the Divine level where souls reside.

One might well ask, if this is true, then what about the vast numbers of people who fail to meet up with their soulmate here on Earth and remain single or get divorced, either through choice or circumstance? The explanation is that they could have met the person intended for them, but failed to recognize them – often for psychological reasons such as fear. Also, the current misplaced emphasis on fending for ourselves could be a self-imposed form of shutdown, cutting us off from a spiritual unfolding through partnership. In some extreme cases, it may even be possible that we somehow 'miss' our true partner through being born at the wrong time, while the soul waits to be reunited in another life.

What about the concept that we should constantly bear in mind the Divine relationship? Ideally, a kind of balancing act occurs, where accord between man and woman and within the family is a way of ensuring the pathways to the Divine are kept clear. This does not mean that we have to keep 'real' emotion down and sweep bad feelings under the carpet. Judaism has a nice way of ensuring that anger is expressed but is forgiven as being part of the *yetzer hara*, the evil inclination. This 'evil' is inherent in everything that is Divine. While it is present, though, it is as if we have created a partial eclipse of the sun. So, while we can acknowledge bad feelings in relation to our families, the sense is that the good and the harmonious are always there if we can allow everything else to pass away and pull ourselves back in the right direction. *Shalom bayit*, peace in the home, is a fundamental aspiration. Even though Judaism in its practical wisdom acknowledges this situation may not always be the case, it can be sought out as a place of return. Knowing that whatever you do is somehow part of a spiritual structure as well as a personal one, that everything has consequences for God as well as yourself, is what keeps the believing Jew on the path of relationship harmony even when times get tough.

Jewish life also has specific inbuilt rituals for acknowledging what others mean to us and to feel, through this emotional love of family, love on a higher level. The Friday night prayers said at home include the recitation of praise by a man for his wife and blessings for the children.

JEWS AND SEX

Sex is regarded in Judaism as a powerful force. At its highest spiritual level, sexual intercourse symbolizes the union between God and the *shekhinah* – the feminine aspect – and thus produces Divine harmony. At its most extreme this belief brought about the practice of concentrating on Divine unity while making love and disciplining oneself to take no personal pleasure in the act itself. This would ensure that the more spiritual aspects of sex would become released and the baser area of human lust be annihilated. Such was the practice of the esoteric masters, dedicated to controlling the physical being so they could induce the reign of the spiritual.

The way of most ordinary Jews was and still is to enjoy sex within the context of a relationship, deepening bonds and experiencing perhaps the closest to the ecstatic state through orgasm. The Baal Shem Tov, the original Hasidic master, saw the bliss of sexual ecstasy – most supremely between a man and wife on their wedding night – as our own tiny foretaste of the bliss of Divine unification in the higher worlds.

Sexual conduct is subject to certain regulations and requirements. Most important are the rules of what is called 'family

100

purity', where sexual contact is not allowed while the woman is menstruating and for seven days afterwards *(see below)*. Masturbation also carries strict warnings, although its interpretation is loose. 'Spilling seed' is more justifiable when it is for mutual enjoyment than as a voluntary emission. The prohibition is more to do with wasting the vital force, the creative function of which reflects that of God in engendering new life or harmonizing male and female. The Rabbis who formulated these rules were also concerned that as a solitary activity masturbation caused separation and reduced the need for a vital partnership.

Sex between couples has not generally, in Judaism, been sin-laden. It is a life-enhancing activity, at best our closest thing to spiritual unity. Only in the rarer examples of religious extremism has it been a matter for suppression and repression. All aspects of sexual behaviour were discussed by the Rabbis and sensible principles set out in the *Talmud* and the writings of Jewish philosophers. They show a healthy regard for harmonious sexual relations – a man is told to approach his wife with care, to be concerned with her sexual satisfaction and not to deny her conjugal rights. Couples are warned against having sex while feeling angry with one another or after having too much alcohol.

In observant circles what look like extremes of sexual modesty are required. Women are traditionally expected to comply with strict rules of dress, including covering their head once married. Is this – one criticism from non-observers – another version of male dominance? The argument from women who keep this law is that it enhances their own sexuality within their chosen relationship. Displaying sexual messages (hair is a vital one) keeps them 'on display' and vulnerable. Women can feel more in control of their own sexuality by limiting who they reveal themselves to. A culture of modesty also ensures that men and women are not so jaded by constant sexual messages that their own partners cease to have an impact on them.

Do Jews condone sex before marriage? Today only the most orthodox circles where early marriage (around 18) is the norm expect virgin brides and grooms. Most Jews, even where they carry out the *mitzvot* regarding the purity laws and other norms of sexual modesty (as in Modern Orthodox) have experience of sex before marriage, albeit between committed couples expecting to become life partners.

CYCLES OF ABSTINENCE – WOMEN AND RITUAL PURITY

Sexual contact is not permitted for around two weeks of the woman's menstrual cycle, although how far this is carried out between modern couples is debatable.

At the end of the *niddah*, as the abstinence period is called, women go to the *mikveh*, a ritual bath, where they are immersed in running water and recite a blessing before returning home. Sexual relations can then be resumed until the next period. Women are also *niddah* after childbirth because of the flow of blood and, if they are virgins, after the marriage night, because of the bleeding following the piercing of the hymen. There is a move to abolish this marriage *niddah* among modern orthodox women who say that it is a frustrating start to the partnership. The argument for it is that it allows a gentle introduction to sex and gives the couple the chance to harmonize their emotions after their first sexual contact.

Many people, however, feel the purity laws are completely outmoded and have never experienced the ritual, which is largely confined to observant couples. The monthly *niddah* is looked at with horror by those who don't practise it and with satisfaction by those who do. The divide has much to do with the translation – 'impure' – and the suggestion that women are sent into a kind of purdah by men in fear of and as punishment for their menstrual bleeding. Actually there is a variety of deeper meanings for the ritual, which is said to be extremely valuable, even to the extent of keeping marriages together and sex interesting. As with many customs, although the original impulse arose out of spiritual necessity, it became eroded and distorted through the ages. Certainly feminists have a case that male control came into the picture at some point and the 'pollutedness' of women was a theme brought to extremes and fostered by fear in the Middle Ages.

The female retreat from active sexual life for half of her cycle is to do with her contact with the darker forces of life and with death itself. Blood, sacred in ancient cultures, is our contact with the essence of life and death. Menstrual blood has a particular potency. At the time of menstruation women are in touch with death, experiencing the loss of potential life. The time is treated with respect in primitive cultures and menstrual taboos originally had more to do with mourning and rebirth than with male supremacy. Contact with death is said to render the living 'impure' in many societies, and the laws of menstrual impurity are part of this process of defilement and re-emergence. Translated into mythology, it is a 'descent' into the darker parts of the soul, a retreat from the physical world into darkness. If women obey their true instincts, many feel, too, that they enjoy this 'time off' without the intrusion of male energy.

For this separation period couples do not to sleep together, and have no physical contact. Those who observe the custom claim that without physical touch, they renew contact in other ways – there might be more time for discussion and family life. The laws of purity also run counter to male domination. In restraining sexual activity, women find they are not slaves either to their own desire or to male demand.

The time when a couple renew sexual contact is important. It is a time of heightened excitement after abstinence, when couples reaffirm their sexual relationship after separation. As one observant women says, 'Taboo and holiness are tied together intimately – the setting up of limits makes what happens within them very special.'

THE MARRIAGE RITE

In line with Judaism's view of relationship, a Jewish bride and groom are encouraged to regard their marriage as symbolizing the union of the *sefirot*, causing purposeful alignment at cosmic levels. They also hope to be partners for life and to build a Jewish home together.

The marriage ceremony itself consists of two parts. The *kiddushin* (sanctification) is the placing of the ring – which must be the property of the groom – on the bride's finger. The ring symbolizes the spiritual ring within which both are encircled. The *nisuin*, the marriage, consummates the sanctification. Bride and groom stand under the wedding canopy (*chupah*) and the bride walks around the groom seven times. The canopy is a symbol of covering the bride and groom in preparation for the physical consummation of the marriage. There are echoes here of ancient fertility rituals and also the number seven is symbolic in Judaism as the number of creation. The *ketubah*, the marriage contract, is read out and seven blessings are recited. The blessings are to do with joy, love and the bliss of the Garden of Eden which the bride and groom are hoping to enjoy. Yet a wine glass is stamped on by the groom to break it, in order to remember the destruction of the Temple and that even amidst rejoicing there is the possibility of sorrow.

A marriage can take place anywhere, and often does. Orthodox weddings usually take place outside a synagogue, so as not to echo the Christian practice of marrying in a place of worship. A festive meal, with music and dance, follows the ceremony and it is considered a great *mitzvah* to create happiness and joy for the couple.

Bride and groom are supposed to fast on the day of the wedding, up to the festive meal, so as to prepare themselves spiritually for their union. It is customary for them not to meet on the wedding day until they see one another under the *chupah*. The bride is also veiled in memory of the betrothal of Rebecca, whose face was covered when she first saw Isaac. Usually the couple spend time alone in a private room immediately after the ceremony. This is a time of sanctity which has an especially enhanced meaning if the couple are observant and have not enjoyed private time together before.

Procreation is not mentioned in the Jewish ceremony. It is understood that the couple intend to have children and indirect reference to the sexual act is considered immodest.

The wedding contract, the *ketubah*, first came into use at the time of the Babylonian exile. Originally it was for the protection of the wife and stipulated sums of money to be paid on termination of the relationship by divorce or death. The original prenuptial agreement, it was an important part of the cultures of the time. Currently it is seen as a covenant between the couple, pledging them to each other. Some authorities maintain that the *ketubah* should be reread at times of stress in the marriage, reminding the couple of the strength of their initial feeling.

BREAKING THE TIES

While seeing marriage as the ideal, Judaism has always allowed that relationships are sometimes unhappy and in such cases, divorce is desirable. It is seen as a kind of release, after which both people are free to find their true partners.

Jewish divorce is based on humanitarian principles. It is at heart a no-fault decision, with both parties having to give their consent and releasing one another in a Rabbinical court, if no means of reconciliation can be found. Rabbinically approved conditions for divorce traditionally included refusal to consummate the marriage, impotence, unwillingness of the husband to support his wife, refusal of intercourse by either party, refusing to migrate should the other party want to and finding the other suddenly repugnant due to their contracting a disease. Thus there has never been a precedent for making it hard to divorce should the couple wish to do so.

There are many difficulties, however, if the husband refuses to grant a divorce. The man has to formally apply for the bill of divorce – the *get* – and have it delivered to his wife in the presence of two witnesses – that is, officially he has to divorce her. While the two are in agreement, there is no problem with this. People have found the divorce procedure, no matter how painful, helpful because it is a formal ritual procedure. The *get* is dropped into the wife's palms (removing from it any sense of affectionate presentation) and then cut at the four corners. The *get* itself is kept by the Rabbi and the couple given a legal statement of divorce.

Where the husband fails to consent to the divorce, though, a woman may remain legally bound and unable to remarry for the rest of her life. A wife can also refuse to accept a divorce. While there has always been some relative sensitivity towards the needs of women (the *ketubah* was originally a protective document and the *get* itself required the man to consider his position and not divorce his wife at will), there is now increasing dissatisfaction with this situation. There is agreement that Jewish law must accord with the times and ways are being looked at to alter the bias in divorce while still adhering to traditional principles.

In the past Jewish people traditionally married other Jewish people. Communities were close knit and outsiders viewed with suspicion. Intermarriages have always increased in cultures of assimilation, however, including the present. Nowadays the question is both how to prevent intermarriage and also how to deal with it when it does happen.

Basically marrying someone outside the faith is not encouraged among Jews. Even the most assimilated still feel that it is preferable to be with a Jewish partner. This has more to do with sharing a common cultural heritage, coming from like backgrounds and having the same world view than anything to do with religious views and spiritual practices.

Observant Jews, would never entertain the idea of being with someone non-Jewish because it contravenes Jewish law. Besides that, the whole Jewish way of life, when practised observantly, is too rigorous for anyone from outside to cope with easily. Although couples of different levels of observance do manage to live together, it is not simple because the hows and whys of Jewish practice are deeply personal issues pertaining to the way we think and feel as well as what we do. Thus being with a partner who is essentially living outside all these issues is not really a partnership at all.

Being in a wholly Jewish couple is considered more sound because it ensures a foundation of similarity rather than risking the tensions of dissonance. Judaism is not just a religious 'hat' – it tends to have an emotional and spiritual undergrowth that is hard to quantify. For that reason it is hard to become attuned in the deepest sense with someone without that same background, no matter how much understanding and good intent are on offer.

There is also good reason for maintaining a Jewish family structure. The Jewish people are diminishing in numbers and the Holocaust brought the real possibility of them dying out altogether. It is a more difficult job to maintain Jewish ties and identity where only one half of the partnership is Jewish, and with little commitment and education it is hard for children to know who or what they belong to. Thus the Jewish community is concerned to keep intermarriage to a minimum.

Where it does happen – and it is estimated that one half of all Jews will marry out – the attitude is mixed. Orthodoxy believes it is best to ensure it never happens, but in the wider Jewish world the drive is to include the non-Jewish partner and if at all possible encourage them to convert to Judaism. It is said that a person who is interested in Judaism and who is drawn to being with a Jewish partner has within them a Jewish soul which somehow became lost.

Judaism does not encourage proselytes – the conversion process is long and difficult (rather less so in the Reform movement, although orthodoxy is unwilling to accept Reform conversions). A heartfelt desire expressed by the non-Jewish person, without coercion, to take on Judaism will be fully tested out in practice – and active discouragement is often the first step. But if the person shows commitment and perseverance, eventually they will be accepted and welcomed into the Jewish faith.

WORK AND REST

And Heaven and Earth and all their host were completed; then
with the Seventh Day, God completed His work which He had
made, and with the Seventh Day He ceased from all of His work
which He had made. And God blessed the Seventh Day and made
it holy, for with it He had ceased from all of His work which He,
God, had brought into existence in order to continue the work of
creation upon it.

GENESIS 2:1

Traditionally there is no great work ethic within Judaism.
More emphasis is placed on how to rest than on how to
work. This may sound strange – does it mean Jews are
inherently lazy, taking as much time as they can for self-
indulgence? Not really. In Judaism the 'day off' – Saturday,
Shabbat, the Sabbath day – is not a time for letting your hair
down and doing whatever you fancy. Together with the festivals, it is sacred time. It is not seen as a holiday, but a 'holy day'.
It is a period when you reject the workaday world in favour of
the spiritual, when you create divisions in order to detach from
what is profane and reach for something quite different.

Most Jews nowadays live in the everyday world. Some live outside it, in strictly orthodox circles in Israel, London and New York. The most fundamental of Jewish sects believe it is undesirable to have any contact with secular life, as its whole premise is at odds with theirs. While there is a genuine fear of contact bearing contamination (the strongly religious separatists are known in Hebrew as 'frightened ones', whether in fear of God or mankind), the religious orthodoxy would say there was no point in communication, because a secular outlook was of no interest to them. More and more, though, observant Jews choose to live and work in a secular world without compromising their values.

There is no Divine commandment to work as there is to observe the day of rest or keep the festivals. Work is simply a means to an end, a way of supporting a family and imparting certain values to one's children. Yet all the great Rabbis and philosophers of Judaism have had trades to sustain them. Rashi, the Talmudic commentator, was a vintner in France. Maimonides, the medieval philosopher, was a (often overworked) physician in Egypt. There are records of learned Talmudic Rabbis being scribes, leather workers, sandal makers, bakers and grave diggers. There are injunctions to teach sons an honest living, but preferably to shy away from 'unpleasant' trades (tanning or camel driving were cited in the Rabbinic period!) Most highly valued are jobs which help others and the community, and in particular affect future generations.

Traditionally Jews were an agricultural people, later learning trades which could be transferred to new lands. In medieval times certain trades became forbidden to them, and land ownership also became restricted – so Jews became associated more

with intellectual pursuits and indoor activities. Countering this tendency, some Rabbis have stressed the benefits of physical effort. The idea of generating a whole new breed of Jews thriving on tilling the land came into reality when Jews started returning to Palestine in the early twentieth century. Jews became outdoor people, exemplified by the *kibbutz* movement – collective farms based on the socialist ideal.

In ultra-orthodox Jewish life, however, work has come second to study. The theme has been that the material world is there to support the spiritual and the way to attain the spiritual is through study.

In Eastern Europe study was highly valued – propounded by the fact that economic conditions were so restrictive that Jews could rarely take pride in their working life. It became the norm in many cases for women to carry on the everyday business of earning a living – running market stalls or small shops in their own home, sewing or tailoring – while husbands studied *Torah* and *Talmud*.

EVERYDAY ETHICS

There has always been a strong ethical dimension to the Jewish way of life. Moral principles have been enshrined in Jewish law and teaching from the times of the great Rabbis and sages when the whole Jewish pattern of life was being formulated. Often it is in joint ethical values that Jewish people find a common unity – even when they are divided about different levels of religious observance.

Modesty and honesty are highly regarded, as are compassion and justice. Jews have always been enjoined to deal kindly and their neighbours and business associates – there are many examples in the *Torah* extolling kind acts and the details of how to do them, which the Rabbis expanded on. You are supposed to extend hospitality to others, to praise the virtues of other people, to visit the sick and those in mourning and to act to save life.

Charity is also a requirement of Jewish life with each Jewish person expected to give according to his or her means – one tenth of your earnings is suggested. Gossip and spreading scandal are also frowned upon – Jews are warned to 'guard the tongue' and not to harm anyone with words. Kindness to animals is also advised, as are general 'acts of justice' and a balanced path in life.

SHABBAT AND THE JEWS – A SACRED MARRIAGE

The idea of Sabbath is deeply imbued in the national Jewish consciousness. Keeping *Shabbat* is a starting point when people are becoming more observant. The Jewish Sabbath has a deep spiritual appeal. Historically it was important, a day when you could leave behind a life of very real toil and live on a different level. Even though its intent is serious the Jewish Sabbath has never been a day of dreary solemnity. More, it is supposed to be affirmative, joyous and pleasurable on physical, emotional and spiritual levels.

There is a kind of dual celebratory mood to both Sabbaths and festive days. On one hand you are enjoined to supply yourself with all that is most pleasurable to the senses – fine clothes, the best food, warmth and comfort. In the past even the poorest of people would save some scrap of good food or a piece of new clothing for *Shabbat*. But the idea is not to stop at that. These enjoyments are just a gateway, a means of appreciating God in the world. It is said that on *Shabbat* a person gets a second soul. Their higher self attends them, enabling them to experience things in a different way. Senses are heightened – food tastes better, the garden looks greener, life takes on a changed quality. Those who take Sabbath observance on board say they experience the quality of real peace and a deep sense of spiritual refreshment.

The Sabbath day is said to be God's particular gift to the Jewish people. On it they affirm that he alone created the universe and that his rest day belongs to them both. A story about the Sabbath says that the day complains to God that all other days in the week have a partner while it is alone. God replies that the congregation of Israel is its partner – and thus, Israel is married to the Sabbath day. This imagery of the Sabbath as a bride of Israel has been taken up by Jewish mysticism and also worked its way into the classical tradition. The Sabbath is personified as a beautiful woman, to be welcomed and enhanced, fragrant and adored. Hymns are recited as if to a bride, a queen or a lover.

In kabbalah the Sabbath is taken a step further. Not just mystically symbolic, it is the actual force of the *shekhinah*, the female principle. Joining in ritual combination with it will create a unity which gives us the chance to experience the bliss of God's unity, beyond all divisions and splits. The Sabbath is said to be the ideal time for men and women to have sexual intercourse, because they will then help in bringing about unification on a higher level. If they conceive at that time, it is especially propitious, and will draw down a special soul to occupy the new body.

If God is the acknowledged creator of this world, he is also seen in Judaism as asking the people to assist in completing creation. The day of rest is our reminder that God left his creation in its incomplete state. His work finished becomes ours to start. The Sabbath day brings this to mind and commits us to the holy partnership.

The Sabbath day, more than any other day of the week, is actually full of restrictions. For a day which should bring joy and delight, it imposes on us so many rules and regulations that it might seem that the opposite is true.

It is indeed a conundrum. Rather than allowing us to do what we please, we have to do what the requirements stipulate. Instead of doing nothing, it is a day when observant people actually have *more* to do. What happens in practice is that the rules enable you to 'switch off' the work routine, and thus create a different space. The restrictions are there to free you from the mundane, the profane, from everything that is not part of God's world.

It is very often pointed out that modern life, instead of giving us more 'freedom' and enjoyment, has enslaved us to money, technology, schedules and deadlines. A 'holiday' from the stress of everyday life is considered essential from time to time. Going to sleep or lazing on a beach may be useful, but deliberately cutting yourself off from the whole ethos of the everyday is valuable for mind and spirit as well. Sabbath restrictions mean you don't go shopping – so are free of financial concerns. You don't drive a car, cutting out the stress of being on the road. You don't travel far from home, and so change your rhythm from rushing to get from place to place. Cooking is not allowed – so, there is more time to savour food you have deliberately prepared beforehand. You don't carry things outside of a stipulated area – thus, there is a great freedom in doing without the usual heavy bags we drag around in daily use. There is no writing, which frees us from associations with all forms of work. Electricity is not turned on or off – thus we can be more attuned to the rhythms of natural light and dark (modern homes use time switches which allow for the enjoyment of the Sabbath

without sitting in the cold or the gloom). TV and radios are silent, allowing for peace and quiet or inner contemplation – or personal communication and discussion. There is no gardening, cleaning, mending or making – none of what is considered 'normal' weekend activity. What then do Jews do? They let go – and contact a different source of life force.

Sabbath regulations are not arbitrary. Like everything else in Judaism, they are stipulated by the Rabbis who laid down the rules in order to make the bald *Torah* obligations more doable by the general populace. A commandment simply to 'keep the Sabbath day' didn't mean much – it was open to as many interpretations as there were individuals. So the Rabbis of the early centuries after Christ formulated interpretations for the people, but at the same time they made sure the central precept was kept intact by surrounding it with 'fences' – things you had to do so there was no chance of contravening the main requirement.

For this reason, work disallowed on Sabbath (and to a large extent festivals) is divided into several categories. There are 39 of these, many reflecting the times when they were first set out (eg, sowing, spinning and slaughtering animals). The Rabbis based the categories on the types of work involved in the building of the Sanctuary. Yet all of modern life is incorporated too, because each of these categories contains the most minute indications for everything we might do today. The category of sowing for instance is defined as 'inserting a fertile vegetable object into a place where it may sprout and grow'. Since the object of the activity is to induce sprouting and growth, we infer from that that no gardening might be done. The 'fence' around this obligation is that no pips – say from fruit that one may eat – should be dropped onto bare earth because they might possibly take root. This is known as an 'impermissible result of a permitted act'.

When it comes to essentially modern activities, each is examined according to its processes. Sometimes the definition can be tricky. The direct use of electricity is banned on the basis of several categories – it might come under 'building' or 'demolishing' because of the connection of positive and negative poles, although primarily it is 'kindling', that is any operation which creates a spark. Since 'bringing something into being' is an overall condition for prohibition, turning electricity on and off is certainly a Sabbath 'no'.

Over and above the minutiae of what is allowable and what is not, it is more meaningful to look at the purpose behind the rules. *Shabbat* is basically about keeping you away from creative acts. We stop ourselves from bringing new things about, from altering or changing anything, in honour of what God did when he desisted from creation. Thus the definitions of 'work' are not strictly to do with work but with creating. This gives us a new place in itself in which to use ourselves, reflecting God himself on the seventh day when perfect tranquillity reigned. In contrast to the seeming negatives of what we can't do, the most important commandment is the positive one – of resting on this day in harmony with God.

With this in mind, many modern Rabbis speak more of the spirit of the Sabbath than of the strict requirements of the day. If you view it in the light of a deliberate freeing up from everyday things, easing the everyday load, it becomes easier to embrace the rules not as burdens but as aides. Few modern Jews believe they will be struck down by God if they fail to keep the commandments – or be rewarded in heaven if they do. Observing the rules of *Shabbat* is thus no longer a matter of obedience to authority, but spiritual self-help. Jewish tradition simply tells you to take action first, and then to see what happens. Keeping *Shabbat* is a way of letting something different happen. Ultimately it gives you the experience of another way of life out of bounds of the ordinary.

MAKING IT SPECIAL

What are the usual ways of making a special day? Some practices are almost universal amongst Jews as a way of 'making *Shabbat*'. The Sabbath and the Festivals all begin at sunset of the day before. In the Jewish world Friday was traditionally an extra busy day, spent cleaning and cooking. Today you are still supposed to make extra special efforts to prepare the home and yourself – as if in expectation of a special guest, the Sabbath spirit. Making adequate preparation, it is said, ensures a Sabbath that is the true foretaste of the World to Come.

Candles are lit at home at a designated time well before sunset – in order to avoid possible infringement by leaving it to the last moment. Blessings are said when lighting the candles, and also over wine and bread. The evening synagogue service inaugurating the Sabbath includes the 'Welcoming of the Sabbath Bride', in which the congregation turn in the opposite direction for the last verse – the custom originated by the Safed kabbalists, who used to go out into the fields in order to greet the Sabbath. When you come home from synagogue on Friday night, an angel is said to accompany you. Also traditional in Safed, kabbalists would gather together and each give account of their week in a kind of spiritual 'confession'. This is often taken up in contemporary gatherings where each one may assess their own week and relate what has been personally important.

Meals play a particularly important role on *Shabbat* and on Festivals. On *Shabbat* you are required to have three meals, all containing different food. The first meal is the Friday evening one, when traditionally families eat together. Food both adds to the festive pleasure and is supposed to echo the taste of the Divine world. The second major meal takes place on Saturday at lunchtime, and the last is eaten prior to sunset. This third meal is said to be the most holy of all – traditionally it was a

time when Hasidic Rabbis would tell stories and their words were believed to be communicated from the *shekhinah*, God's female aspect, itself.

On the Sabbath no gloom is allowed. If you have private and personal needs, this is a day on which they are laid to one side. Prayers deliberately omit all supplications because reminding ourselves of what we lack is contrary to the *Shabbat* spirit. Also in this spirit, we try to be conscious of what we talk about and how we think. Referring to everyday matters, work, money and the like are not 'fitting' for *Shabbat*, and religious Jews will choose their subject matter with care. Mourning is suspended on Sabbaths. It is however permitted to cry – but only if it affords emotional release not if it deepens sorrow.

Saturday is the day when all synagogues hold morning services – both a communal and spiritual function. Central to the liturgy is the reading of the weekly *Torah* portion, a new one starting each *Shabbat* and repeated on Monday and Thursday of the following week. The tradition is said to have originated when the Jewish people came out of slavery in Egypt 3,000 years ago. Their rebellion against God was said to result from failure to remind them of the *Torah* for more than three days – thus, no more than three days has ever been allowed between public readings since!

For many people this *Torah* reading is a chance to re-create your own relationship with the Bible, seeing what personal meaning the week's reading has and keeping in touch with what is happening through the religious re-reading of your people's history. It's also a simple chance to add to your knowledge of the Biblical landscape. Much emphasis is put on the week's *sedra* (reading) and orthodox families discuss it and offer new interpretations throughout the day.

Being active yet creating nothing, learning and wondering without working or striving – *Shabbat* is a unique form of time out, restricting normal life to give room for holiness to enter.

MAKING A SEPARATION

A simple ceremony, at home or in synagogue, marks the end of Sabbaths and Festivals. *Havdalah*, coming from the Hebrew work *lehavdil* which means to make a separation, is a way of making the distinction between the sacred and the profane.

It involves wine, candle and a box of sweet smelling spices. A cup of wine is taken in the right hand – the 'active' hand – and the traditional *kiddush*, the blessing over the wine, is said. This is followed by a short prayer thanking God for making distinctions between the holy and the profane, light and darkness, rest and work. The spice box is passed round, and lastly, when it is well and truly dark, a candle is lit and everyone present spreads out their hands towards the flame before it is extinguished and the workaday world comes forth again.

In the *Havdalah* ceremony all the senses are involved, making us aware once more of our physical selves and drawing us back to normal life from the purely spiritual. We taste the wine and smell the spices, see the light and touch the warmth, and speak the various blessings. The sense of smell is said to be the most mystical and detached from earthly senses. It is particularly emphasised, as the spices, which are said to nourish the soul, are held close one last time before the special Sabbath soul departs for another week.

EATING AND DRINKING

Kashrut can best be explained in our times as a form of spirituality through everyday behaviour among Jews. The Jewish dietary laws draw our attention to eating as a conscious act and remind us of our relationship to the environment, animals and the food chain.

DR DAVID ARIEL

J ewish people are associated with a love of food and drink, and Jewish cooking is known and loved in Europe and America. It tends towards the hearty and sumptuous, and is the product both of austerity and celebration. Jewish people used their food economically and went to great lengths to eke out what they had, but food was also a way of glorifying Sabbaths and festivals and had to be made special on a regular basis. It was to some extent symbolic – many of the festivals have particular dietary customs which serve as a reminder of their spiritual significance. As in many cultures, eating is not just a physical matter, whether of necessity or pleasure. Rites and strictures add another dimension.

Judaism has a complex system of dietary laws, which may seem to restrict gourmet pleasures. True, much of the food enjoyed by the rest of the world is forbidden to Jews. Not only

that, but normal admixtures of food (notably dairy produce with meat) are also prohibited. Perhaps this has caused Jewish people to make especially imaginative use of the food which is available in order to make it palatable. Certainly within the context of firm dietary laws there has arisen a cuisine all of its own. This has taken the cooking of different countries and adapted it to specifically Jewish requirements. Thus you will find Jewish people from different areas cooking with the flavour of the place yet turning it into their own cuisine. So there is Russian Jewish cooking and Polish cooking, Tunisian and Egyptian, Indian and English. The variety in the tradition has also served to keep Jewish food important in world cuisine.

The dietary laws are one of the best known and universally observed Jewish practices. Yet in modern Jewish life, there is a strong divide between traditional orthodox practice and Reform/Liberal on this question. To some extent dropping *kashrut* (the Hebrew term for dietary observance) has been officially sanctioned by liberalizing factions who could not justify it intellectually as a modern practice. They also felt it proclaimed Jewish separateness and militated against acceptability. Changing Jewish demography also meant it was often difficult to get hold of the proper food and so the custom was dropped. Nevertheless, eating in the correct way is not to be taken lightly. As one of God's commandments it forms an important part of Jewish practice and tradition, and, like keeping *Shabbat*, is a growing area of observance by people returning to Judaism.

FIT TO EAT

Jewish food is *kosher* food. The word actually means 'fit', implying that it is both fit for Jewish people to eat according to Jewish law and that it fits the requirements of the *halacha*, the legal code. The word itself has slipped into general parlance, meaning that something is OK, has been sanctioned and is above board. Another word used in relation to food is *kashrut*, meaning the law itself appertaining to fit, clean or appropriate food for Jewish consumption.

What makes food *kosher*? Four factors are equally important: the type of food, the method of preparation, the way of cooking and the manner of eating. Foods permissible for Jews are animals which both chew the cud (i.e. are vegetarian) and have cloven hoofs – sheep, cattle, deer and goats. Most commonly known as being out of bounds to Jews is the pig. Fish must also have two features – fins and scales. This notably excludes all shellfish. Certain species of fowl are allowed, but these have no specific characteristics – there are 24 altogether, mentioned in the Bible, and by default all others, including birds of prey, are *unkosher*. Additionally not permitted are amphibians, insects or creeping or crawling creatures, thus outlawing eel, ant and snail. Food produced from *unkosher* sources is also not allowed – ostrich eggs for example – with the one exception of honey.

The permitted food must then be made fit to eat. *Kosher* animals must be killed in a *kosher* manner. This disallows anything which has died a natural death, been unhealthy or been killed by anything other than ritually approved slaughtering methods. Animals must be killed by a Jewish slaughterer (*shohet*) who is fully cognizant of all the rules of the ritual. A sharp knife is used and as much blood as possible removed. Jewish slaughtering methods have come in for modern criticism because they do not allow stunning before killing. Stunning, however, would injure the animal and thus render it unhealthy before killing. Defenders of *kosher* killing say it is humane because of its immediacy and painlessness.

Certain sections of the animal are also considered *unkosher* – the sciatic nerve, for instance, is not allowed and since it is hard to remove, this law renders much of the entire hindquarters *unkosher*. The prohibition came about in memory of the injury suffered to the vein sinew by Jacob when he wrestled with the angel. Any internal disease found after slaughtering may also make the meat unsuitable for Jewish consumption.

The Jewish concern about impurity through contact with blood extends to that of animals (although blood from fish does not count). Thus all traces of blood must be removed after slaughter through the special processes of *koshering* – washing, salting, soaking in water or broiling. This all used to be the job of the Jewish housewife. Today it is done by the *kosher* butcher. The fat of the stomach and kidneys is also stripped away.

The most important part of the *kosher* kitchen is the stringent separation between dairy produce and meat (which includes fowl but not fish). Dairy (which includes products made with any dairy ingredient) and meat are never eaten in the same dish or at the same meal. Opinions differ over how long the separation period should be between eating one and the other – it can be anything from three to six hours. Although dairy food may precede meat without a time lapse, practising Jews do not have them at the same meal at all. Some items of food are *parve*, i.e. neither dairy nor meat. Thus you can have non-dairy ice cream or cream after meat.

This separation does not stop merely at the food. All cooking utensils, cutlery and crockery must be kept strictly separate. Orthodox households have separate kitchens or areas of the kitchen (particularly the sink) for dairy and meat. For reasons of upholding *kashrut* religious Jews will not eat in restaurants where milk and meat items are not kept separate.

At the most intricate levels laws governing what is and what is not *kosher* are rather movable. The strictest Jews have their own Rabbinic governing bodies which decide on what is allowed, so often food that even one observant Jew will eat will not be fit for another.

Like other activities we share with animals, the process of consuming food can be sanctified and raised to a different level. Thus there are certain ways of making us conscious of God even in this mundane everyday occurrence.

Jews are commanded to make blessings both before eating and afterwards. Hands are washed before a meal (anything which includes bread constitutes a meal), but this is not just a hygienic scrub – it is a ritual, one hand pouring water over the other in remembrance of the strong assisting the weak, accompanied by a blessing to God in acceptance of this commandment. After hand washing it is customary not to talk until the next blessing has been said – to God for 'bringing forth bread from the earth' – and a piece of bread has been eaten. Keeping silent is a way of staying in touch with the holy nature of the procedure rather than interrupting it with everyday chatter.

After each meal grace is said. This can be done communally, and usually is on festive occasions and Sabbaths. On ordinary days usually each person takes a few moments to go through the grace privately, from memory or a prayer book. The grace after meals reminds us that God is the provider of all things and will bring redemption to those who deserve it.

The Rabbis of the past were insistent on maintaining a peaceful and holy atmosphere in which to eat and it is recommended that the level of conversation around the dining table does not deal with mundane or contentious issues. The table has been compared to the altar of the holy Temple – Jews should feel the same while eating as they did when offering the holy sacrifice. Eating food is indeed a bridge between death and life and being aware of its import keeps your actions in touch with who or what presides over humanity.

The regulations regarding *kashrut* come directly from the Bible. They are specified in the books of Leviticus and Deuteronomy: Leviticus 11:2–47 and 7:23–7; Deuteronomy 14:4–21. There is also passing mention of 'clean and unclean' animals in Genesis 7:2 and 9:3.

In fact, the first mention of God instructing man about what to eat comes in Genesis 1:29. Here vegetarianism seems to be advocated, with seeds yielding vegetable life and trees bearing fruit deemed to be food for mankind. This has been interpreted as being the ideal diet, but later compromise was made on account of the 'craving' for meat which our animal self has. Thus the idea is that if we have to eat meat, we should at least make it an act of special significance so we behave as rather more than just animals.

Even though the laws of *kashrut* are clearly defined in the Bible, what has proven rather problematic is that there are absolutely no explanations as to why they were set up. We are simply told this is how it is for the Jewish people. Keeping to the laws is therefore a matter of blind faith. It is because they don't seem to make much sense that Jews have attempted to make sense out of them with a variety of rational explanations, none of them entirely satisfactory. Ultimately many Jews have dropped the dietary laws entirely, because of failing to find justifications for them either to themselves or the non-Jewish world.

HEALTHY OR HOLY?

What, then, are the reasons why so many Jews *have* stuck with these inexplicable requirements? Some of the more practical explanations have been made on historical grounds. Jews, it has been suggested, were attempting to do something more humane than the pagan custom of tearing limbs off animals before they ate them. The prohibition on mixing milk with meat may have been derived from Egyptian times. Milk signifies life, meat death. The Egyptian culture centred around death, therefore separating life symbolically from death in eating was a way of affirming Jewish culture on a different basis from that of the Egyptians. Another possibility is that since blood and the fat of the stomach and kidneys were used in Temple sacrifice, they were considered taboo for human use. The use of only vegetarian animals has been linked to a Jewish distaste for violence and blood sports. The early Rabbis also suggested that aversion to cruelty was behind the biblical injunction – repeated three times for emphasis – 'not to seethe the kid in its mother's milk' leading to the rulings against the mixing of the two food groups.

Modern justifications for the dietary laws have centred around their health benefits. Pigs and shellfish have been cited as 'unclean' in the sense that they are likely to impart disease, and dairy produce and meat require different processes in the stomach so may provide an indigestible mix. Maimonides himself, who was trying to find reasons to satisfy perplexed medieval Jews, said that pigs were dirty animals. Although this kind of reasoning was a way of defending the dietary laws, it also provided a good rationale for *ceasing* to observe them. Pigs can indeed be very clean in their habits and modern production methods supposedly ensure that food is 'fit' to eat.

But the dietary laws are really nothing to do with health or hygiene, nor do they necessitate putting ourselves in the mind-set of biblical people in order to be appreciated. A clue to how they should be regarded is in the exact translation for prohibited and permitted animals – *tamai* and *tahor*. These are words used very specifically, within the context of religious ritual, with the connotation of religious purity and spiritual defilement. Thus *kashrut*, rather than just being a matter of simple cleanliness, is actually linguistically associated with a high level of sanctity.

The importance of *kashrut* is also underlined by its place in *halacha*, Jewish law. The law has four categories and *kashrut* falls into all of them. First, it is a reflexive law because it causes something to happen within ourselves when we do it. So in one way *kashrut* is for ourselves. Like keeping *Shabbat*, no one is watching us with a big stick to see we do it right. But doing it gives a sense that life entails segregation and that we have to bear in mind the higher separation between good and evil, sacred and profane. *Kashrut* causes us to be mindful of how we go about the simplest of tasks – each time you go to eat you have to stop and become more aware. Keeping *kashrut* also instils large amounts of self-discipline. Abstaining from prohibited food is not supposed to be easy. One is supposed to want it but to desist consciously from eating it.

The dietary laws also come under the ethical heading, because they help us become aware of how we kill and eat our food. They influence the way we regard slaughter of living things, and create an attitude of mind and spirit towards the blood of life.

Kashrut is, too, a national law. It helps people to identify with those Jews who carry it out and to commit to their community. It constantly makes people feel Jewish, both when they are out and when they are at home. It separates the Jewish people, both for their good and, some have argued, to their detriment – and is an ever-present reminder of who they are.

Lastly, but just as importantly, *kashrut* is one of the laws of holiness, which raise the ordinary to the spiritual. Followed with full devotion, *kashrut* elevates the act of eating and transforms it into something more than just mindless physical satisfaction.

So, seeing the dietary laws as mere practical measures misses the point. They are in fact some of the most mysterious of the

Jewish practices. There is simply no way of knowing why this particular set of rules constitutes *kashrut*, or why we have to keep them. Yet *kashrut* is one of the practices that starts from blind faith and somehow reveals its own personal significance as you go along.

FOOD FOR THE SPIRIT

The special occasions of Judaism are full of rituals to do with food. While famous dishes such as chicken soup, chopped liver, *gefilte* (chopped) fish and smoked salmon all have their origins in necessity – eking out poultry, meat and fish and salting for preservation – other foods have more spiritual connotations.

The festival of Passover has the most complicated of food rituals. Nothing which contains leavening of any kind is permitted and this is not such a simple matter because not only all foodstuffs but also the utensils which touch them have to be separated. This requires stringent cleansing of the home, especially the kitchen.

The easy explanation of this ritual is that it is performed in memory of the rapid departure of the Jewish people from Egypt, when they had no time to leaven their bread. There are other levels of understanding too. Leavening is associated with self-pride and the evil inclination, and the enormous lengths Jewish families go to in order to remove all traces of it are supposed also to act as a form of self-cleansing and purification.

Instead of ordinary bread, *matzah*, which is flat and unleavened, has to be eaten. All other foodstuffs should also be especially *kosher* for Passover, i.e. guaranteed to have been kept away from normal foods during production.

The Passover ritual *Seder* – a family celebration of prayer, singing and retelling the Exodus story – has food as a main feature. Food is greatly symbolic on this occasion. A plate with

ritually laid out items is central to the table throughout the (often long) festivities. It contains green vegetables (usually parsley) to symbolize rebirth at this spring period. A sweet mixture of apples, nuts, wine and spices known as *haroset* represents the mortar with which the Jewish slaves made bricks for the Egyptians. Ground up horseradish (*maror*), strong and bitter, is a reminder of the bitterness of slavery. An egg within its shell, roasted till black, is offered in memory of the Temple sacrifice and as a universally symbolic part of spring festivals. A scorched piece of shank bone acts as a reminder of the special Passover sacrifice – the Pascal lamb – which used to be offered in the Temple rite. Lamb itself is never eaten at Passover in deference to the fallen Temple and its sacrificial rituals.

During the meal itself it is customary to eat egg with salt-water – a symbol of the tears of slavery and the renewal of freedom. Four glasses of wine are required to be consumed during the course of the evening (grape juice, as a 'fruit of the vine', blessed beforehand, is also acceptable). Four is the esoteric number of repetition and the whole Passover *Seder* is a repetition of the story which Jews have told as one of their primary myths for all generations.

Shavuot, Pentecost, an early summer festival, is associated with the eating of dairy dishes. The festival commemorates the giving of the law at Sinai. The *Torah* in which the law is enshrined is often compared to milk and honey, and dairy produce keeps us in mind of this. It also reminds us of the reception of the laws of *kashrut* and the segregation of milk from meat, which was more commonly consumed.

The autumn festival of *Rosh Hashana*, the New Year, is inaugurated with apples and honey to express the desire for a sweet season. Other sweet foods, such as honey cake and sweet vegetables like carrots, are also traditional at this time. Fruit is eaten to enable you to say a blessing for new produce of the season. Bread is baked in rounded shapes to signify the completion of a cycle. Fish is eaten, particularly the head, as the 'head' of the year. Oriental Jews use an animal head.

Although *Yom Kippur*, the Day of Atonement, is a 25-hour fast, food plays an important part both before and afterwards. A sustaining meal is prepared to eat prior to fasting and completely different foods are served to break the fast.

At *Hanukah*, the midwinter festival, it is traditional to eat dishes containing oil in memory of the oil which burned for eight days instead of one, keeping alight the candelabra in the Temple which the Jews were attempting to save from defilement by the invading Greeks in 167 BC. Potato fritters and doughnuts are popular, as is a rich steamed fruit pudding, perhaps a slight cross-cultural fertilization!

During *Purim*, in early spring, triangular pastries filled with a sweet poppy-seed mixture are traditional. They supposedly commemorate the hat of Haman, the villain in the biblical story of Esther. Another association, with Haman's ears, may stem from very early versions of the story, perhaps originating in Mesopotamia prior to 600 BC, and the sacrificial rites of the time.

The Friday night meal at the start of the Sabbath is also important. It is a time when especially fine foods are served. Two *challot*, sweet bread enriched with egg, must be used for the blessing prior to eating, commemorating the double portion of manna which the Jews received on the Sabbath while wandering in the desert before they entered the Promised Land. Due to the prohibition against cooking on Shabbat, a heavy stew known as cholent, generally consisting of beans, potatoes, barley and meat, is left on a low heat overnight and eaten for Shabbat lunch.

PART III

SPIRITUALITY IN THE CYCLE OF THE JEWISH YEAR

T he Jewish calendar works on the lunar cycle. Since the moon's cycle is about 29.5 days, Jewish months may have either 29 or 30 days in them. Normally there are 12 months in the year, but that means they are short of the solar year by 11 days. To keep both more or less together, and to ensure that the festivals are kept in their appropriate seasons, an extra 'leap' month is added at what amounts to seven times in each 19 years – i.e., every two or three years. This month, Adar II, occurs in early spring.

It is said that the second month of Adar has a powerful but fickle and temporary nature. It is a 'pregnant' month, when things are given a chance to happen but can equally easily be erased. If bad things happen in the second Adar, they happen just so you can have that experience, with no lasting consequences.

The festivals of the year are set in their Hebrew dates, but these will vary from year to year in the secular calendar. Sometimes, for example, the New Year, *Rosh Hashana*, may be in early September, but it can be as late as October.

There is also a discrepancy between the holy days as celebrated in Israel and in the Diaspora. During the Second Temple period the new moon, on which the month started, was announced by the high court in Jerusalem when eyewitnesses actually saw the moon appear in the sky. It was hard to tell precisely when this would happen – two consecutive days were possible. It was also impossible to let far-flung Jewish communities know in time on which day the moon had been sighted. Thus a system arose in which Diaspora Jews celebrated two days for the beginning of a festival, in order to cover all possibilities. Only *Yom Kippur*, the 25-hour fast, was exempt. *Rosh Hashana*, the Jewish New Year, is also different because it is celebrated for two days everywhere. Various rituals were set up in the Diaspora to cover both festival days and so the old traditions remain, although modern movements have questioned their necessity.

Also different in the Jewish cycle is that each festival and *Shabbat* begins at sunset (when the first stars are seen) and ends at the next sunset. This practice comes from the Creation story in Genesis, which states: 'And it was evening and it was morning.' In fact the inauguration of Sabbaths and festivals is up to an hour before sunset, in order to leave no room for error.

The cycle of festivals is intimately bound up with stories from Israel's past history. Each festival is not just a holiday but also a time of spiritual refreshment, ritual acts and rekindling the past. Also requisite is a preparation time. Some holidays take weeks of advance planning and activity, with Passover being the most time-consuming. The holidays can also be taken on a very personal basis. Like the cycle of weekly readings from the *Torah*, they reflect and impinge on your own personal story and past history.

The festivals are also based around ancient rites, both the agricultural ones of the Near East and those of the times when the Temple was still standing in Jerusalem, a place of pilgrimage and sacrifice. Over the years since then the stories have been retold and the rituals re-enacted, with alterations and additions according to changing times. The cycle of events of

132 the Jewish year thus reflects nature and the origins of mankind, incorporates the whole history of the Jewish people and has deep echoes of personal and family significance.

The Hebrew year is numbered differently from that of the secular calendar. In ancient times the year was numbered from 'year one' in the reign of a new king (or possibly the date of a special event in that people's history). When another memorable occasion supplanted the last, the yearly counting restarted from the beginning. Thus, in the Christian era, we have the years starting from year one of the birth of Christ – with nothing so far important enough to reset the clock.

Judaism, however, since it does not accord Christ such distinction, has not restarted its yearly cycle since the supposed date of the completed Creation. We are thus in the sixth millennium. This may not be scientifically accurate, but it has been suggested that the seven days which Creation took were stages equivalent to millennia. Regardless of trying to make faith fit with physics, the date has the spiritual significance of tying the Jewish people to God's master plan.

Ta'anit ha'B'chorot (Fast of the Firstborn)	14 Nisan	March/April
Pesach (Passover)	15 Nisan	March/April
Shavuot (Feast of Weeks)	6 Sivan	May/June
Ta'anit ha'Shiva Asar Tammuz (Fast of the Seventeenth of Tammuz)	17 Tammuz	June/July
Tzom Tisha b'Av (Fast of the Ninth of Av)	9 Av	July/August
Rosh Hashana (New Year)	1 Tishri	September/October
Tzom Gedaliah (Fast of Gedaliah)	4 Tishri	September/October
Yom Kippur (Day of Atonement)	10 Tishri	September/October
Sukkot (Tabernacles)	15 Tishri	September/October
Simchat Torah (Rejoicing of the Law)	22 Tishri	September/October
Chanukah (Dedication/Festival of Lights)	25 Kislev	November/December
Tzom ha'Asara Tevet (Fast of the Tenth of Tevet)	10 Tevet	January/February
Tu Bishat (New Year for Trees)	15 Shevat	January/February
Ta'anit Esther (Fast of Esther)	13 Adar	February/March
Purim (Feast of Lots)	14 Adar	February/March

PILGRIMAGES

> Three times a year – on the Feast of Unleavened Bread, on the
> Feast of Weeks, and on the Feast of Tabernacles – all your males
> shall appear before the Lord your God in the place that He will
> choose. They shall not appear before the Lord empty-handed, but
> each with his own gift, according to the blessing that the Lord
> your God has bestowed upon you.
>
> DEUTERONOMY 16:16–17

There are three pilgrim festivals in the Jewish calendar –
Pesach (Passover, the Feast of Unleavened Bread), *Shavuot*
(Pentecost, the Feast of Weeks) and *Sukkot* (Tabernacles).
All are intimately connected. They are the oldest festivals in the
Jewish year, having clearly evolved from ancient agricultural
rites to do with the land and the harvest. Prayers said at all
three include references to their seasonal nature and all bear
connotations of wandering and search, impermanence and
shelter. They draw attention to the human desire to both settle
and roam, to seek the spirit and to find a home.

In the past, pilgrimages were made to the Temple in Jerusalem. The most important was the Passover pilgrimage, when
the Pascal lamb was offered up, although we do not really know

whether every male in the land of Israel made the journey or whether this was just a suggested ideal.

After AD 70 the site of the destroyed Temple became a place where people went in order to get in touch with its holy nature. Nowadays the Western Wall in Jerusalem is a popular place of pilgrimage. Said to be the remaining wall of the Temple itself but actually part of the wall around the Temple Mount built by Herod in the first century BC, it is imbued with faith, hope and prayer.

PESACH – PASSOVER

Passover begins at full moon on the fifteenth of the Hebrew month of Nissan. It lasts for seven days – eight in the Diaspora. Its name comes from the story of the plagues which God visited on the Egyptian people when the Pharaoh refused to let the Jewish slaves go. God told the Jewish people to put a sign on their doors so that the angel of death would 'pass over' their houses when the command was made to kill all the firstborn.

Preparations for the festival start weeks in advance. The home has to be cleared of *hametz* – literally, a mixture of flour and water that has been allowed to ferment and rise. What this means in effect is that every crumb must be sought out and removed – which means a deep cleansing ritual that surpasses any normal spring clean. Parcels of *hametz* are symbolically burned just before the festival. Although the cleaning ritual is done according to strict *halacha* –Jewish law – the rules are constantly brought up to date, even as far as cleaning microwave ovens is concerned. After the cleaning, special utensils and food for the festival are brought into use.

The first and last days of Passover are holidays on which normal work is not permitted. However it is not quite so strictly regulated as the Sabbath – cooking for instance is allowed, as

long as it uses an existing light. At the start of Passover a prayer for dew is recited as part of the synagogue service, recalling life in the land of Israel where the dry summer is about to begin and also the whole agricultural nature of the festival. The intermediate days are semi-holidays. Some people use these days to do festive things – in Israel the week of Passover has a holiday atmosphere. Then Passover is completed with another full festival day.

Passover has many symbolic levels of meaning. It is above all a festival of liberation. It is fundamentally a spring festival, based on ritual celebrations of the rebirth of the year. Yet it is also attached strongly to one of the most predominant Hebrew myths, that of the coming out of the land of Egypt. So the liberation from winter has become transformed into liberation on a cultural and spiritual scale.

In the Hebrew myth Egypt itself can be seen as symbolizing the antithesis of the spiritual life, with its emphasis on death and pagan ritual which involved appeasing a variety of gods. The Jewish Exodus was therefore not just a physical freeing from hard labour but also a spiritual liberation. The people were now able to take on themselves the covenant with one God, to behave according to moral principles and to become responsible for acting with God.

The Passover festival is inaugurated by the *Seder* (meaning 'order'), which retells the story of the Exodus from Egypt. The *Seder* is a gathering which normally takes place in the home for family and friends. It can seem like a strange mix – part dinner party, part religious service, with songs, games, discussions and chatter, sometimes festive and solemn, sometimes full of conversation and jokes.

The story retold at the *Seder* is both a personal journey and a communal event. It has the flavour of a family tale and indeed it is supposed to be aimed particularly at children. Four set questions about the Passover are asked by the youngest child present and everyone at the table is encouraged to become involved in answering them. It is the job of the leader of the *Seder* to find creative ways of making the story interesting and immediate.

Everyone present should feel what it was like to be part of the Exodus – and, through that, to know what it is like to go from a situation of enslavement to freedom. To bring the ritual into the personal realm, each person can find a way to focus on what their own form of slavery is, whether physical routine or psychological attitude, and then seek liberation from it.

The *Seder* story is essentially of what God did for *us* when we came out of Egypt and we not only remember it but also re-experience it through what is almost a dramatic re-enactment. The Passover ritual has a unique way of realigning us with the Jews of long ago and keeping us in close relationship to them. It allows us to feel a historical connection with each generation which has told this same story. The *Haggadah*, the book from which the ritual *Seder* readings come, tells us that each person in each generation should feel as if they are being personally redeemed. Inherent in the story is thus not just a review of the past but also hope for the future, when the world itself will be redeemed and freed from evil. At one stage of the *Seder* service Elijah the prophet, traditionally the herald of the Messianic Age, is welcomed.

Even the most secular Jews tend to hold a *Seder*, especially in Israel where there is a large secular majority. To non-religious people the ritual gathering to tell the story and eat the meal still has traditional and cultural significance, rather like Christmas dinner.

The week of Passover is a time when you are constantly reminded that something out of the ordinary, different from the rest of the year, is going on. Food is completely different, with no leavening allowed *(see p.127)*. This means no bread. Instead flat crackers are eaten which have a guaranteed minimum

period of contact between water and wheat so that no trace of rising can occur. Ritual foods are not just there because they are nice to eat, but to serve as reminders of the strong symbolism behind them. The ban on leavening is not just a historical link to the generation who, the story goes, left Egypt with no time to allow their bread to rise, but also a symbol of what it is like to do without luxuries and on a psychological level of letting go of being 'puffed up' with pride and self-importance.

Although the rules of Passover are very strict, the effect is similar to that of *Shabbat*. You store away all the things you normally use (orthodox Jews even sell them on a temporary basis) and the hard work of separating things off, of deeming some things suitable and others out of bounds, ensures that those which are used are special.

So the festival acts as a liberation in its own right – a liberation from normal everyday things and mindless daily activities. It reminds us that we can do without our addictions – and that we can become free, as the Hebrew people did, with God's help.

SHAVUOT – THE FEAST OF WEEKS

The Feast of Weeks (also translated as Pentecost) is an early summer festival, celebrated on the sixth day of the Hebrew month of Sivan. The festival occurs at the end of the period of the *omer*. The *omer*, which means a 'measure', was the first new grain of the harvest and it was brought to the Temple at the beginning of Passover. From that time, the Book of Leviticus says that a count of seven weeks should elapse, then on the fiftieth day another sacred offering be made. The time of the second offering is the date of *Shavuot*.

In orthodox practice this period of counting has taken on an esoteric nature. The time between Passover and Pentecost is a spiritual preparation, the multiple of seven that makes it up having special significance and reflecting the lower seven *sefirot*, those appertaining distinctly to the human realm. A spiritual practice you can do each day involves focusing on one aspect within the broader context of the *sefira* of that week. For instance, in the week during which the governing principle is lovingkindness (*hesed*), the theme for the first day would be seeing the pure love within love, on the second day the judgement and power (including anger) within love, on the third the beauty and splendour in love, and so on. The system can be used both externally, in how these qualities are manifested in the world around you, and psychologically, in how you experience them in your own psyche. At the same time you should also work with the consciousness of trying to balance these qualities in both spheres so as to create harmony and balance.

Shavuot, which follows, can then be experienced in a balanced spiritual state so that one is ready to relive what it really represents – the giving of the law at Sinai. In fact the connection between the date and the historical event is somewhat spurious. The Bible itself makes no reference to the events at Sinai being celebrated by the festival of *Shavuot*. It was simply a rite marking the end of the grain harvest, onto which the later connection was grafted.

The festival took on its modern form after the destruction of the Temple in AD 70. At that time there could be no ritualized marking of the grain harvest and there was also the necessity to set a formal date for remembering the Covenant at Sinai. This supposedly happened during the month of *Sivan* and so was fused with the ancient festival date. On *Shavuot* the Book of Ruth is read in synagogue, both for its agricultural connections and harvest images and because it represents committing and cleaving to a peoplehood.

Shavuot is a holiday on which no work is done. It has special food rituals – mainly dairy dishes are prepared and eaten – so it is certainly a time for feasting. A custom which comes from six-teenth-century Safed kabbalists is to stay up all night and study selections from the Bible, Rabbinic and mystical literature. The custom is supposed to heighten your spiritual consciousness so you are ready for the Revelation. As at Passover, the festival is more than a holiday, it is a re-enactment. It also acts as an atone-ment, because traditionally the Israelites had to be woken by Moses in order to hear God. Now we make sure we stay awake! It is also said that *Shavuot* is the wedding of Israel with God. Staying up helps to prepare the bride. In Israel the custom is to converge on the Western Wall to pray at sunrise.

The *Torah* reading for the morning of *Shavuot* includes the Ten Commandments. Some communities decorate their home and synagogue with green plants, both recapturing the agricultural image and that of the *Torah* as the 'Tree of Life'.

Shavuot is a time of the culmination of many desires and images. We specifically eat bread in memory of the harvest offering, in contrast to Passover when we are restricted in preparation for the physical and spiritual journey. At *Shavuot* we are allowed full nourishment, in both a worldly sense and the spiritual one of taking on the teachings of the *Torah*. The fes-tival is a reminder of the Covenant and of the renewed option to take on its obligations. It brings us up against the spirit of the golden calf, when the people forgot God's words and turned to alternative worship, and we wonder how far we are doing this today. It shows how liberation from enslavement is not enough in itself – you have to take on the codes and disciplines of free-dom in order to lead a full spiritual life. *Shavuot* also reveals the cycle in mankind's relationship with God. At times high and full of clarity, it then comes down to Earth, as Moses did from Sinai. Once more the voice is not so present or all-commanding and you are diverted, as the Hebrew people were, into false means of fulfilment.

The third pilgrimage festival, *Sukkot*, comes in autumn, after the high holy days – the New Year and the Day of Atonement. In biblical times it was highly important and known as 'the festival'. The Temple rituals at that time were very elaborate and there were numerous sacrifices each day. In Messianic times *Sukkot* is said to be the festival which all people will celebrate.

After commemorating, in the former pilgrim festivals, the Exodus from Egypt and the reception of the law at Sinai, the festival of Tabernacles recalls the wanderings of the Jewish people in the desert before they finally entered the land of Israel. Agriculturally, it was the final harvest of the year.

Sukkot lasts for seven days, like *Pesach* having its important festival days at the beginning and end and the days between as semi-holidays on which work may be done. In terms of the calendar it is the direct opposite to *Pesach*. Each can be seen to reflect the other, containing inverse qualities and bringing to light contrasting features. *Pesach* is said to teach the existence of the Creator and *Sukkot* to prove his continuing presence.

Sukkot is a happy holiday, even though it comes second only to *Pesach* in the hard work and preparation involved. It is a specific *mitzvah* to enjoy the festival. Central to it is the *sukkah*, a small shelter which has to be temporary. It is built at the side of your home then deconstructed. You are supposed to live in the *sukkah*, although nowadays people mostly interpret this as eating in it and occasionally sleeping in it, weather permitting. The Rabbis strongly outlawed spending time in the *sukkah* when it was raining, as it was not supposed to be associated with discomfort.

There are strict rules appertaining to the building of the *sukkah*. It is supposed to be built of branches, poles and other natural materials and most important is its roof, through which

you should be able to see the stars and the heavens at night. The *sukkah* is meant to be beautiful. A motley collection of items can be considered suitable decorations: pieces of cloth, fruit, sweetcorn, pictures, prayers, paper chains are all possible. Traditionally the building of the *sukkah* starts immediately after *Yom Kippur*, turning solemnity into festive joy.

Sukkot is therefore about construction, building a home in the wilderness even though it will need to be left at any time. Rather than just being looked at and talked about, as at the *Pesach Seder*, at *Sukkot* our symbols have grown to enable us to surround ourselves with them. The *sukkah* thus gives shelter not just to the wandering people, but also to the symbols of the Jewish spirit. One Rabbi of Talmudic times, Eliezer, said that the *sukkah* had a purely non-physical meaning – it represented the clouds of glory which protected the Israelites in the desert and which were either God's actual presence or the sign that he was present. The *sukkah* is therefore both a symbol of impermanence and of spiritual shelter. It signifies trust in times of spiritual wandering and security even when you are homeless.

One custom connected with the *sukkah* is inviting in *ushpizin* – guests. As at Passover, those in need should be remembered and offered hospitality in the form of food and wine. As well as real guests, symbolic ones are also important invitees. They include the great biblical figures such as the patriarchs – Abraham, Isaac and Jacob, Moses, Aaron and David. Modern updatings include matriarchs on the list. The idea is to commemorate their greatness and invite some of their spiritual quality to join you and stay throughout the festival. Kabbalists also believed that each guest represented an aspect of God and would bring the significance of that quality to the day.

Sukkot has one other unique distinguishing feature. For the festival one should have in one's possession 'four species' – specifically, a citron (*etrog*), a palm branch (*lulav*), two branches of willow (*aravot*) and three myrtles (*hadasim*). The basic procedure concerning these four is to hold them and shake them in six specified directions during the prayer service. The same can also be done in the *sukkah*. The four items should be firm, fresh and intact. It is essential to check that the dried stem of the *etrog* – its *pitom*, or point – is in place.

There is a variety of explanations for this seemingly bizarre custom, whose Jewish nature was probably grafted on to much earlier pagan harvest and fertility rituals. The four species have been said to symbolize four types of Jews (those with learning, those who perform good deeds, both of these or neither). They have been compared to parts of the human body – the straight palm branch for the spine, the myrtle the eyes, the willow the mouth and the citron the heart – thus making up a whole. They have been linked to the masculine and feminine, and seen as receptors of Divine energy. They could relate to the Garden of Eden – traditionally Eve was said to have eaten the citron, not the apple. The myrtle has many spiritual associations in both Judaism and Islam. It is used in wedding festivities and the *havdalah* spice box *(see p.118)* and the prophet Isaiah says that it will grow to herald the return of the people to Zion in the Messianic Age. The order of shaking the species in six directions is reminiscent of the aspects of space from which all matter came as expounded in the early mystical work, the *Sefer Yetsirah*.

The four species are also carried around the Ark of the synagogue in a circular procession. A special hymn, the *hoshana* (meaning 'save us') is recited in the procession, during which the Ark is open and a *Torah* scroll left out. This happens on each day of *Sukkot* except the Sabbath. It is a direct recall of the procession around the altar in the Temple.

The three pilgrim festivals form and complete a cycle. In the first, at springtime, we are offered spiritual involvement. At the

144   second, approaching high summer, we are told the terms of this involvement. And ultimately, in the autumn of the year, God shows the extent of his spiritual involvement with his people.

FASTS

Is such the fast I desire, a day for men to starve their bodies? Is it bowing the head like a bullrush and lying in sackcloth and ashes? Do you call that a fast, a day when the Lord is favourable? No, this is the fast I desire: to unlock the fetters of wickedness, and untie the cords of the yoke to let the oppressed go free; to break off every yoke. It is to share your bread with the hungry, and to take the wretched poor into your home; when you see the naked, to clothe him, and not to ignore your own kin.

ISAIAH 58:3–7

Fasting has gone on from time immemorial as a spiritual activity. Historically it was a form of penitence, used to inflict a sense of personal deprivation so we were more likely to feel our errors and to ask for forgiveness. Fasting was also a form of petition. In times of great hardship it was a way in which people could do something to convince God that they were serious and worthy of his input into their affairs.

Fasting also has personal spiritual effects, ones that hold true in the modern world. Temporary starvation brings you close to your own mortality. It has, too, always been one of the quickest ways to achieve a genuine change of consciousness. When you fast not only are you physically enabled to leave behind the

concerns of the everyday routine, but you also become more attuned to the non-physical world.

The object of a fast is not to get through it as quickly as you can. Although it is very hard not to think about food, the whole idea is to elevate and concentrate the mind so that the spiritual becomes paramount. Even though a degree of difficulty and self-discipline accompanies a fast, once you get through the initial discomfort food almost becomes an irrelevance.

Fasting can also have a social and ethical value. We are put in touch with how it feels to be hungry and thirsty – perhaps for the only time in our lives. The fast can therefore stir the conscience to do something to help the less fortunate during the rest of the year.

In the Jewish year fasts also have a commemorative function, keeping the present generation in touch with the events of the past in a personal way, rather than having former disasters confined to dusty history.

Most people when they think of a Jewish fast day think of *Yom Kippur*, the Day of Atonement, which is the best known and most celebrated. *Yom Kippur* is, however, but one of seven fast days in the Jewish year. Admittedly, not all are kept and most are probably unrecognized by the majority of Jews, and some authorities think the minor ones should be phased out altogether. But each one has a different character and flavour, emphasizing varying aspects of the Jewish past and encouraging different reflective frames of mind.

Jewish fasts are both private and public affairs. The major fast days are a bonding activity for the community, drawing together all who take part in the shared experience. On a private level, each individual experiences a fast in a different way. All the Jewish fasts are supposed to bring about private reflection, personal realization and changes in behaviour. At most they are Judaism's most dramatic way of achieving a spiritual 'high' unprecedented during the rest of the year. The fast experience may also differ considerably from year to year, sometimes being intensely meaningful and at other times hard to appreciate.

Fast days should not be regarded as all doom and gloom. Serious as they are, the point is also to have an opportunity to start again. You look at yourself, your life and history, and end the day knowing that spiritual renewal is a reality. Within the withdrawal and the pain, joy is never far away.

YOM KIPPUR – BEING AT ONE WITH GOD

The Day of Atonement is the culmination of 10 days of repentance, which starts on the New Year, *Rosh Hashana*. It is a particularly solemn time, which has aptly made a transition to modern terms as an opportunity for introspection and forgiveness, resolution and self-development. 'Atonement' has been neatly redefined as 'at-one-ment'.

More Jews celebrate *Yom Kippur* than anything else. Even if eating *kosher* is anathema and *Shabbat* just another day, *Yom Kippur* strikes a chord in the memory and behaviour of every Jew. In Israel it is a day of near-total shutdown in private and public life.

The day started out, though, as a Temple ritual which brought God extraordinarily close to the people and when the high priest made atonement for the whole community. It was on this day only that God's name – unknown today – was pronounced in public by the high priest. This must have been an act of extraordinary power, which we may compare with an esoteric chant which could affect energy on many different levels. The day's ritual also had the effect of cleansing and purifying the Temple, without which the Divine presence could not enter. The ritual of the high priest, which included his selection of an animal to be killed as a 'scapegoat' for the sins of the people, is a central part of the modern afternoon service. The precise account of how this was done is read from the prayer book and the community performs a symbolic re-enactment where they kneel to the floor at each of the four times the high priest's confession is made. The ritual is not only to do with the priest – it is also his own commemoration of Moses' meeting with God at Sinai. The import of the occasion is therefore enormous and the whole congregation symbolically joins with the sense of spiritual upliftment.

The whole of *Yom Kippur* is a day of prayer, usually in synagogue, with just a short break mid-afternoon. One is supposed to abstain from all normal, pleasurable things as well as food and drink – expressly, sexual relations, wearing leather, bathing and 'anointing with oil', nowadays interpreted as putting anything on your skin, so make up and shaving are prohibited.

It is traditional to wear white on *Yom Kippur*. This is supposed to remind you of your own mortality, white being the colour of the burial shroud. Secondly it is the colour of purity, from the passage in Isaiah where scarlet sins will become 'white as snow' after true repentance.

On the evening when the fast begins, the extremely solemn *Kol Nidre* prayer is chanted. This is a formal declaration that we may have gone astray in the year just gone, we may have failed to keep promises and drawn back from our commitments. It is a sign that we will look anew during the following day at our shortcomings and seek to redress the balance.

On the morning of *Yom Kippur* you are supposed to get up early – the day has to be used intensively. The idea is not to sleep the day away in idle rest! *Yom Kippur's* prayers are full of confession, repentance, pleading and hope. The continuing themes are of judgement and remorse, but that should not make the day heavy going. Amidst all this is the knowledge that we have a chance during this special time out from the world to see where we have gone wrong. Then there can be a return to the way God wants us to go.

On *Yom Kippur* the Hebrew liturgy is repeated over and over, time becomes immaterial, and the quality of the ongoing chanting is hypnotic, meditative, introspective and expectant. Doing without food and drink is supposed to make you become like the angels, who have no physical needs.

In the afternoon there is a special reading from the Book of Jonah. The story of the errant people of Ninevah shows that it is possible for a whole city to find its way back to God, that there is a compassionate God and that we cannot escape serving God.

There is a gradual increase of intensity during the day, concluding in the *Neilah* service. The prayers of this service are full of emotion, imploring the Divine to look kindly on us, hear the heartfelt voice, know our inmost desires and allow us spiritual sanctuary. The imagery of this sunset time is imperative, referring to the 'closing of the gates', which is taken to mean the gates of Heaven – and could also have been the physical closing of the Temple doors. The day ends dramatically with short, urgent chants and the triumphant blowing of the *shofar*, the ram's horn.

In a sense *Yom Kippur* is a process, beginning with the preparation during the days before it and building during the day's concentrated prayer. It is not supposed to be encountered suddenly, straight out of ordinary life. Beforehand it is helpful to consider, at least for some time each day, how we have behaved during the year and the ways in which we want to change ourselves. Particularly appropriately, we should ask forgiveness before the day from anyone we might have hurt or harmed. This clears the time of *Yom Kippur* itself for the process of reconciliation between oneself and God.

Nowadays *Yom Kippur* has become a time not for focusing so much on 'sin' and 'repentance' as on personal change. It has many qualities which seem intensely meaningful. In the face of something higher and greater, we also face ourselves, our own

spiritual possibility. We know there is a way to leave the past behind and to go forward.

MOURNING AND REMEMBERING

TISHA B'AV

The second most important of the fast days, Tisha b'Av, is on the ninth of the month of Av. It is a major fast day, like Yom Kippur, lasting from sunset to sunset.

The day recalls the two major historical destructions of the Temple. While there is no accurate documentation attributing this date to the first event, it is believed to have happened during the Hebrew month of Av. The Second Temple, though, was almost certainly burned down on the tenth of Av, but the conflagration began the previous day. Since the ninth was already a fast day, fixing the date of the first destruction, it was now additionally loaded with sorrow.

Another historical connection is with Moses' spies who went into the land of Canaan and came back declaring that it would be impossible to conquer, thus demoralizing the Israelite people.

Subsequent events piled the date with more sadness. It commemorates the Roman destruction of the last Jewish uprising, the expulsion of the English Jewish community in 1290 and the final expulsion of the Jews from Spain in 1492. The First World War also began on the ninth of Av. The time of the year itself could also be a 'black period'. In the Middle East it is high summer and a time of drought, when the land itself looks charred and infertile. Thus the ancient Israelites could have seen it as a barren desolate time when help was needed to bring God back from hiding.

In fact the fast day is preceded by a three-week mourning period. During this time there are no celebrations and no wedding ceremonies. Pious people do not take wine or meat in memory of the Temple sacrifice and also to abstain from luxury.

In the week of *Tisha b'Av* one of the readings from the Bible is taken from Isaiah. This is the passage where the prophet rebukes the people for their sins in his most severe voice and warns that disaster is coming. The evening before the fast the meal is particularly frugal, consisting of egg, the traditional mourner's dish. Shoes are sometimes left off and people do not greet one another.

In synagogue praying takes place in semi-darkness. The prayer leader (and others if they wish) sit on low chairs, like mourners. The liturgy is chanted with a plaintive air and the whole atmosphere is one of quiet mourning. Everything is kept as plain and unadorned as possible, and the Book of Lamentations is read, recalling national sorrow and communal responsibility.

Yet the mood is not wholly sorrowful. There is within the festival a sense of hope. The sad time is only temporary and from its ashes we will arise stronger and more peaceful. It is said that the Messiah will be born on *Tisha b'Av*, thus joy will come out of sadness.

GEDALIAH – MURDER AND WASTE

After the destruction of the First Temple in 586 BC by the Babylonians, many of the working-class people were left behind in Judaea instead of being taken as captives to Babylon. Nebuchadnezzar wanted these Jews who had been left behind to have a stable government so they would not make trouble. Gedaliah ben Achikam, a prominent Jew and a follower of the prophet Jeremiah, was put in charge of them.

The neighbouring country of Ammonites, however, became scared that Jews might again rise to power in Judaea and had Gedaliah killed. Some versions of the story say that the Jewish

zealots of the day also had a hand in the murder. Many Israelites, fearing retribution from Babylon, fled and some were taken off to Babylon.

This date thus mourns the laying waste of the land and the end of that period of hope for a strong Jewish presence in Israel. Penitential mourning prayers are read.

THE TENTH OF TEVET – ANCIENT CATASTROPHE

The fast of the Tenth of Tevet was originally in memory of King Nebuchadnezzar of Babylon's siege of Jerusalem. During it, prayers for forgiveness are read, as is the story of the golden calf, recalling how the people's strayed from God's word and thereby brought upon themselves national catastrophe and disaster. This is one of the four fasts which specifically marks the destruction of the Temple in Jerusalem (others are the seventeenth of Tammuz, the ninth of Av and the Fast of Gedaliah). Jews remember the fall of the Jewish state of old, their historical swings of fortune and attempts to influence them, and the nature of what is temporary and what is lasting.

SEVENTEENTH OF TAMMUZ – THE LOW POINT OF SUMMER

We can't be sure what this fast commemorates. It could be to do with the Babylonian entry into Jerusalem during the final days of the First Temple or it could be the start of the Second Temple disaster. As with the ninth of Av, several other events have been added to it. The first tablets of the law were destroyed by Moses on this date when he found the people worshipping the golden calf. It was also the time when Syrian Greeks under Antiochus were trying to defile the Temple and the last date on which Temple sacrifices were performed.

The day itself is a minor fast, when you only have to go without food and drink from sunrise to sunset and work is permitted. It marks the beginning of the period of three weeks leading to the ninth of Av. During the Sabbaths of these weeks, passages are read from the Prophets, describing the destruction of the community both physically and spiritually.

Although high summer, this is religiously a low-key period of general restriction. During this time we think of the state of exile, in modern times translated as the loss of a strong spiritual centre within. We feel how far we are from the presence of God.

MINOR FASTS

ESTHER'S VICTORY

This date, the thirteenth of Adar, just before the festival of *Purim*, commemorates the story of Esther, who pleaded to the Persian king, Ahasuerus, to rescind an order of massacre against the Jews. The Book of Esther records that she requested that the Jewish people fast with her for three days before she went to the king in order to gain spiritual strength. The fast may also be in memory of the defence of the Persian Jews and their victory over their enemies. Its liturgy expresses the hope that the Jewish people will be removed from all suffering with the help of God. The fast is not generally observed today.

This fast was originally held later, in the month of Nisan, when *Pesach* occurs. The date was 'Nicanor Day', commemorating a victory of the Maccabeans, and was a joyous festival. Later it was considered inappropriate to hold a fast close to *Pesach*, so this date was chosen.

The fast is now kept as a reminder of the salvation of the Jewish people and of victory over destruction. Like all the other fasts, apart from *Yom Kippur*, it is brought forward if it happens to be a Saturday, because fasting on either the Sabbath or Friday interferes with *Shabbat* joy.

The day before Passover is officially entitled the 'fast of the first-born', but is not actually observed as such. Instead, all firstborn – both male and female – are expected to attend the morning synagogue service, although in practice females are not obliged to do so.

This 'fast' may have come into being to remember the first-born who were killed in Egypt and from that, we can extrapolate, the innocence of people who are overcome by evil regimes. It can also be a form of atonement for those firstborn Israelites who were in fact sinners but whose lives were saved.

RENEWALS

The judgement usually thought of as the end of time is here placed in the immediate present. And so it cannot be the world that is being judged – for where could the world be at this very present? It is the individual who faces judgement. Every individual is meted out to his destiny according to his actions. The verdict for the past and coming year is written on New Year's Day. The year becomes representative of eternity. In the annual return of this day of judgement, eternity is stripped of every trace of the beyond, of every vestige of remoteness; it is actually there, within the grasp of every individual and holding every individual in its strong grasp. There is no more waiting, no more hiding behind history. On these days the individual in all his naked individuality stands before God.

FRANZ ROSENZWEIG

There is one New Year festival in Judaism, but four New Years. All of them are referred to in the *Talmud* as 'judgement days' and those kept today are festive but have an underlying solemn meaning.

Originally, different practices in the ancient Near East allowed some communities to celebrate the New Year in springtime and others in autumn. Thus both the first of Nisan and the

first of Tishri are New Years, but now they are simply beginnings of different kinds. The spring New Year was known as the New Year for Kings, recalling the time when the year was counted from the beginning of the reign of a particular monarch. The first of Nisan is also known as the New Year for Months, as Nisan is actually the first month. Now Passover (the first festival of the year) has supplanted this spring New Year in importance and the first of Tishri, the seventh month, has become *the* New Year – the New Year for Years and the commemoration day of the Creation.

To make matters more complicated, there are two other New Years in the Jewish calendar. Elul, the end of the summer, marks the start of the year for Tithing of Animals. Shevat 15 (*Tu Bishvat*), which is in late winter, is the New Year for Trees. Thus neatly in the Jewish year all is brought into play in the cycle of renewal – vegetable and animal life, leaders of mankind, our world and its cosmos.

Today only two New Years are really celebrated at all – *Rosh Hashana*, the autumn Day of Remembrance, and the New Year for Trees. Both are opportunities to renew your connection with your spiritual being.

ROSH HASHANA – THE BIRTHDAY OF THE WORLD

The autumn New Year festival is held for two days by Jews both in Israel and the Diaspora. Together with *Yom Kippur*, the Day of Atonement, this festival is the most solemn of the year. These two festivals are not just holidays, they are high holy days. In Hebrew they are called the *yamim noraim*, which translates as 'days of awe'. *Rosh Hashana* is the time when we remember how God's judgement is made. On *Yom Kippur*, that judgement is sealed for the year to come.

The whole Hebrew month preceding the high holy days, Elul, is a time of inner devotion when we begin the process of looking at our innermost thoughts and crucially re-examining our lives. Special penitential prayers are read during the week preceding *Rosh Hashana*. Hasidic stories say that during Elul God makes himself available to us by coming down to our level and shines in our midst. By *Yom Kippur* he has returned to his palace on high.

The New Year itself, the first and second days of Tishri, is called in the *Torah* the Day of the Sounding of the Ram's Horn (*shofar*) or simply the Day of Remembering. During biblical times it was a festival day, but nothing like we know today. It only became known as the New Year in Talmudic times. The day may have supplanted ancient coronation ceremonial days which took place at this time of year – God and king are interchangeable in a lot of the liturgy.

The *shofar*, which has a piercing yet plaintive sound, was used in biblical times to signal the start of *Shabbat* and also to alert people to the special nature of particular days, including new moon and festival days. *Rosh Hashana* is both of these, although when the festival occurs on *Shabbat* the *shofar* is not blown. The *shofar* can be sounded in short, staccato or long blasts – they have been likened to a sobbing sound, cries and groans. There is a broken quality to many notes, echoing the fragmented sense of our own selves, yet the suggestion is that we can once again become whole like the full *shofar* note. The *shofar* is a central part of the *Rosh Hashana* service and even people who choose not to sit through the whole liturgy feel satisfied once they have heard it blown.

The festival begins communally on the Saturday night prior to the actual date, when *selichot* services are held. *Selichot* is primarily a set of forgiveness prayers, praising God for his attributes of might and mercy, graciousness and love, his patience and his ability to punish iniquity. Yet these qualities are not just

those of an unreachable God to whom we must plead. We also need them in overcoming our own weaknesses, therefore we are asking for God's personal involvement as well as his all-seeing justice. This is, if you like, a first approach to God in the process of renewal and return.

The morning prayers of *Rosh Hashana* are long and repetitive. Much of the repetition has been cut out in more liberal Jewish communities. It is there, however, not so much to impress us with its literal meaning but to act as kind of chant. Its aim is to clear the mind so that it rests only on the sound. The qualities of God reverberate through the service and the eventual purpose is to convey his essence.

On *Rosh Hashana* the readings from the *Torah* are about the birth of Isaac to Abraham and Sarah in their old age, and the *akedah*, Abraham's near-sacrifice of his only son. The theme of the first story is of birth out of barrenness and that of the second is of obedience and deliverance. Both are to do with the extraordinary power of perfect faith. In both there is complete unity with the will of God, utter absence of personal ambition. God reigns supreme, the ruler of all things.

Rosh Hashana is about how we can keep on recognizing God as this ultimate power in the universe. God as king is the constant message, bringing us up against what is really in charge of our lives instead of what we habitually allow to have power over us. The festival is all about allowing ourselves to find meaningful ways back to living in the light of God's ways. The service calls this being 'inscribed in the Book of Life' which is closed at the end of *Yom Kippur*. The phrase has an emotive ring. The symbol of a blank sheet, on which all our goodness may be recorded, but which is only available for a short time, is both comforting and stimulating.

Like all the holidays, *Rosh Hashana* looks both to our most personal lives and to God himself. The sense is that we continually move between the two, examining our own humanness yet also searching out our Divine possibility. The mystical tradition sees this quite simply as the choice between good and evil. This choice is our responsibility to make minute by minute, with the days of awe providing an intensified opportunity to fully commit ourselves to getting the decision right. Not, however, that any one of the mystics or leaders has ever suggested the way is easy. We have been given our constantly fluctuating passions for a reason – as a vast challenge which helps us build discernment, spiritual awareness and self-discipline.

One *Rosh Hashana* ritual, in particular, can act as a spiritual and psychological catharsis. It is called *tashlikh* (literally, 'casting'). The physical requirements are that you find a body of water which is flowing rather than still (i.e., a stream, a river or the sea) and throw breadcrumbs into it. The crumbs symbolize your sins. The ceremony has been criticized for two reasons. One, from the very orthodox, is that it makes people think they can free themselves this easily from their wrongdoing, without the need of deeper repentance. The other, from modernists, is that it is an embarrassingly archaic practice which has nothing to do with a meaningful approach to the day.

In fact, with the right attitude of mind, it can be useful to perform such a dramatic ritual in a symbolic way. The way to approach it is to connect inwardly with whatever it is you want to see change in your life and to 'cast' whatever is unwanted away. Sometimes it helps to write down the things you want to be rid of before the festival (on which the *Shabbat* rule of not writing applies) and keep them in mind for throwing out in the cleansing ceremony.

The fifteenth day (*Tu*) of the month of Shevat is a festival dating from Talmudic times. It has been regarded as a minor festival, relating to old agricultural principles regarding tithing (an ancient form of tax). A farmer had to know which day marked the beginning of the new fruit crop so he could know on which dates his tithes were due. Recently, however, it has become more popular, especially in Israel, where it is a pleasant and colourful celebration rather than a full-blown holy day.

Tu Bishvat is the closest thing Jews have to a nature festival, heralding the first fruit of the trees and the start of spring. It has a special connection with the return to the land of Israel and the inception of the state. Before then, the festival had fallen by the wayside and was merely celebrated by eating 'foreign' fruit in memory of the land. Carob was particularly popular – it is a long-lasting tree common in ancient Israel and its dry fruit is easily transported. Carob was also said to have kept the Jewish people alive during the Roman siege of Jerusalem.

Nowadays the agricultural theme is strong. Seven species are associated with *Tu Bishvat*, based on a passage in the Book of Deuteronomy describing the land of Israel as bearing forth wheat and barley, vines, figs and pomegranates, olives and honey. Almonds are also of importance, since almond blossom is one of the first signs of spring in Israel. It is customary to hold celebrations at which all seven species are served.

Trees are also planted on the festival. The New Year for Trees is spiritually significant in the way *Rosh Hashana* is for human beings – it is said God decides on that day which trees will flourish and bear fruit. In this way he is ruler of the whole universe, including nature. The idea also disallows any concept of the 'rule' of nature and natural forces, as in pagan religions.

Tu Bishvat has also become popular because of increasing interest in mystical interpretations. The Kabbalists were particularly interested in the connection between humans and trees – an idea with which New Age concepts of our interrelationship with nature would agree. The original link is made in the Book of Deuteronomy, which says, 'The human is like the tree of the field.' We can see the connection in obvious ways – a tree is upright and endures many hardships, it is nourished by the soil from which it comes and even when it seems to have lost everything it retains the will to come back to life. Kabbalists, however, went further than these simple analogies. They saw all trees as symbolizing the Tree of Life from which God's Divine qualities flowed out into the world. Thus eating the seven species on *Tu Bishvat* was a significant spiritual act.

The Kabbalists of sixteenth-century Safed inaugurated a special *Tu Bishvat 'Seder'* during which they would ritualistically drink wine and eat fruit and nuts. Everything was carefully controlled to have spiritual significance. Ten varieties were chosen, this being the number of *sefirot*. Four glasses of wine were consumed (as at *Pesach*), representing to the Safed Kabbalists the four levels of the created world, from the most mystical one, *azilut*, which is really God's realm, through *beriah*, which is Creation itself, and *yetzirah*, the formed universe, to *assiyah*, our immediate physical world. The last three of these, below the spiritual, which we cannot really experience, were spiritually encapsulated by three groupings of fruit. Food which can be consumed in its entirety, for example grapes, apples and raspberries, represent *beriah*. The next level, *yetzirah*, is represented by produce with an inedible stone in the middle of a soft exterior – cherries, apricots, peaches and olives. Finally comes produce with a hard shell around an edible interior – nuts, pomegranates and bananas. Holiness is represented generally by the edible parts and profanity is in what is discarded. As each group was eaten, readings from the Bible or the *Talmud* were heard.

Tu Bishvat Seders are very often held today. Rather than relating to the different levels of existence, which demands much imaginative power and esoteric knowledge, we can more easily use the species to reflect on aspects of our own personality which are hard and soft, defended or accessible, true or fake.

It is also a time for reconnecting to our own roots, whether that means physically gardening in order to prepare for the flowering season or reflecting on our relationship with where we live and with the land of Israel. The New Year for Trees brings us back in touch with the Jewish people's connection to the soil, lost for many hundreds of years in exile.

WAXING, WANING AND WATCHING – THE MONTHLY MOON

The new moon, *Rosh Chodesh*, is a festival of sorts in the Hebrew calendar. Early on, the first day of each month of the lunar calendar was fixed by simple observation. Witnesses whose job it was to watch for the first appearance of the waxing moon would report to the court of Rabbis on the thirtieth day of each month as to whether it had been sighted or not. If so, the new month had begun, and if not, then it would start the following day.

The calendar was fixed permanently in AD 358. Each month lasts 29 or 30 days, with a second month of *Adar* every few years to keep it synchronized with solar time *(see p.130)*. The months of the Hebrew year all have Babylonian or Assyrian names, brought into use by the Jewish people when they came out of the Babylonian captivity in the sixth century BC.

In the ancient non-Jewish world, in fact, the Sabbath day was at first observed only once a month. Only later was it kept at each of the moon's four phases. During the third millennium BC 'taboo' days were celebrated at new and full moon. No cooked food could be eaten, journeys were not undertaken and no work was done. In Babylonian times these turned into 'evil' days. The Jewish Sabbath altered the quality and regularity of the day and *Rosh Chodesh* took over as the monthly festivity. Thus in biblical times for the Jews *Rosh Chodesh* was accompanied by Temple sacrifice, trumpet blowing, feasting and a public holiday. Its status was close to that of the Sabbath.

Particularly important new moons were the first of Nisan *(see p.156)*, the first of Elul *(see p.156)* and the first of Shevat, which was the original date of the first fruit tithe of the year. On the first of Tishri debts were officially annulled, certain areas of land began their fallow period and slaves were freed.

By the return of the Jews from the Babylonian exile, *Rosh Chodesh* had already lost some of its importance and was a working day. It was decreed that women should be free from working then, probably in respect of the menstrual cycle which, if it was in tune with a natural order, would mean women became pregnant with the swelling of the moon. In folklore the new moon is thought to be a good time to start new enterprises and was popular for weddings.

In the Middle Ages it became customary to have a festive meal at new moon – maybe in memory of the special meal served to the witnesses who first sighted the moon in biblical times.

Nowadays the only vestige of the new moon's significance is in synagogue. The public announcement of the new month which followed the witnesses' sightings is echoed today in the synagogue service. The congregation is informed of the new moon to come and a special prayer recited expressing the hope for blessing and goodness, health and prosperity. Another prayer, the *hallel*, is also recited at new moon. *Hallel* is actually

164   six psalms put together in praise of God's miracles, the waxing
and waning of the moon being one.

Another modern way of celebrating *Rosh Chodesh* is in special
women's groups, where women meet for prayer, study and
discussion.

CARNIVALS, LIGHTS
AND REJOICING

Try to be as happy as you possibly can. There are so many troubles that people have to go through physically and spiritually – trying to make a living, etc. – that in many cases the only way they can make themselves happy is by doing something silly and acting a bit crazy. The whole vitality of body and soul depends on being happy.

You should constantly centre your thoughts on contemplating the root of all things. This is the source of all that is good and all joys. You will feel an overwhelming joy, because when one contemplates this root – which is wholly good – then everything good and joyous is merged into one and radiates with abundant light. Joy is freedom.

RABBI NACHMAN OF BRATSLAVA

All the Jewish festivals are essentially times for celebration and even, as we have seen, those with greatest solemnity have within them the opportunity for rejoicing. There are three times in the year, though, which are specially associated with happiness – joyous festivities on which making merry is not only permitted but enthusiastically endorsed.

In the Hasidic world, especially, people were enjoined to seek out happiness and keep from getting depressed. Sadness was seen as a way of letting in evil, and indeed the Hasidim had great psychological insight as they knew that too much unhappiness could lead to illness and mental imbalance. They believed that the mind had power to enable you to break out of gloom and thus come back to being as God wanted you to be. Two things were important in this task – to do things that changed your state of being and to focus your mental powers on everything that brought about joy.

The festivals provided excellent opportunities for both of these. The three happiest celebrations of the year are today often relegated to being thought of as 'for children', but really they have just as much relevance to everyone with the will to let themselves go. Each has its own flavour and emphasis, and a solemn purpose to it too. Being fully involved in these festivals is an emotional and psychological experience that is good for the soul.

PURIM – THE LOTS ARE CAST

The early spring festival of *Purim* is based around the story told in the Book of Esther. The story is a strange one, more like a comedy or farce than one which can be given serious historical consideration. It goes like this. The Persian king, Ahasuerus, banishes his queen, Vashti, for refusing to appear at a feast where he wanted to show her off. He chooses as her successor Esther, a beautiful Jewish woman, although the king does not realize her origins. Esther has a protector, her uncle Mordechai, who snubs the king's grand vizier, Haman, by refusing to pay homage to him. Accordingly, Haman decrees that the Jews throughout the kingdom be massacred.

Mordechai and Esther seek to rescind this decree. Esther seduces the king with wine, tells him she is Jewish and asks him to annul the decree, which he does. Haman is hanged and

Mordechai and Esther celebrate their victory -- with the slaughter of several thousands of Persians.

Many factors point to the story having a pagan Babylonian origin, far earlier than the Persian period (fifth century BC), although traditionalists refute this view. The story has several elements which are completely out of character with Judaism – drinking, sexual licentiousness and mass slaughter. All of these have been subtly disguised yet still feature in today's celebrations, which themselves have elements of the pagan spring carnival when everyone 'lets rip'.

The name, *Purim*, is an Assyrian word for 'lots'. Casting lots before God was done by both Assyrian and Jewish high priests to give 'yes/no' answers – a form of Divine oracle which was of central importance in New Year rituals, of which spring was one. In the story Esther's petition to change Haman's judgement suggests he was a god whose will decided the fate of the Jews for the coming year. Mordechai and Esther have been linked with the pagan gods Marduk and Ishtar. The machinations between the three were updated to include Greek elements (after 400 BC), which were themselves later supplanted as the story evolved to meet the needs of Jewish monotheism. The end of the story indeed meets the needs of a dispossessed people fantasizing about killing their enemies and emerging victorious.

Classical tradition is understandably embarrassed by *Purim*. It is hard to know when the festival began to be celebrated – some authorities suggest it was in operation by the first century BC. Certainly by the Middle Ages it was 'on the map' of the Jewish year. Its religious significance was by then to do with celebrating God's deliverance and the fact that he can work indirectly (God is never actually mentioned in the story). At *Purim* we also 'blot out' the memory of enemies whose aim it is to destroy the Jewish people – although, conversely, we have to remember to forget them, in a typical *Purim* paradox.

The festival is not nowadays celebrated as a fully-fledged holiday – you are allowed to work and carry on your normal activities during it. All that is required is that you listen to the Book of Esther being read, preferably making a lot of noise whenever the villain of the piece, Haman, is mentioned, to drown out his name. This is normally left to children, who are provided with rattles and given full rein to stamp and shout.

An important part of *Purim* is dressing up. Again, this is now largely relegated to children, but the theme of a world turned upside-down is strong, with boys dressed as girls and vice versa. It is a time, in fact, when normal restrictions are lifted – an authorized letting go.

Wine flows freely at *Purim* (unusually for Jews, who are not known for their love of alcohol) and there is some controversy over whether you are supposed to get completely drunk or just, as a Rabbinic text says, 'redolent of drink'. There is a tradition that you should become inebriated enough to be unable to tell the difference between the wicked Haman and the good Mordechai.

In Israel *Purim* is a time of processions and a carnival-like atmosphere. It meets the need to let go enacted in many societies by communal festivities (Spanish fiestas, the Carnival in Rio, for example) yet holds it in a typically Jewish way within a historical and religious structure. Anything goes – but within limits and disciplines.

Even though *Purim* today is largely a festival for children, there is no reason why adults should not also join in the fun. Skits, spoofs and amateur dramatics are held, with music and dancing, concerts using unusual instruments and an irreverent attitude to tradition. *Purim* is really a Jewishly sanctioned opportunity to let your hair down and have a good time. In the midst of all this, though, the festival has an ethical dimension. There is a commandment to give gifts on *Purim*, particularly of food and wine, and this is to ensure that even the less well-off can join in the festivities.

CHANUKAH – DEDICATION TO LIGHT

The midwinter festival of *Chanukah* lasts for eight days. It is a 'working' holiday – like *Purim*, you are not expected to rest from normal activities. All you should do is light the candles on the *chanukiah* – an eight-branched candelabra with an extra holder in the centre (correctly, not to be confused with the *menorah*, the seven-branched candleholder, though in practice the latter term is often used for the *Chanukah* candleholder too).

Chanukah commemorates another Jewish victory, more historically verifiable than that of *Purim*. The Greek invasion of the Near East, under Alexander the Great, took place in the fourth century BC. After the Greek empire fell apart, Israel was controlled by the Seleucids – Hellenized Syrians, i.e., Syrians who had adopted Greek culture. The Seleucid king, Antiochus, ruled in 167 BC that all the people under his control should become Hellenized too. That meant certain unacceptable changes for the Jews. Especially, Sabbath observance and circumcision were no longer allowed, Greek gods were to be worshipped and – the ultimate desecration – pigs were to be allowed in the Temple as sacrificial animals. Some Jews were happy to take on Greek ways, admiring their dedication to bodily strength and physical beauty. Many more were not so enraptured. The crunch came when one of the Jews, willingly taking a pig to be sacrificed, was murdered by a Jewish priest, Mattathias. He and his sons began a campaign against the Syrians and eventually one son, Judah the Maccabee, took over as leader. He and his band (known as the Maccabees or the Hasmoneans) managed to defeat the army of Antiochus and eventually even brought the Temple back to its correct usage. The miracle of the oil, to which

Chanukah is directly related, occurred when the one small vial of oil in the newly purified Temple, enough for one day, continued to burn for eight. The name *Chanukah* is translated as 'dedication', meaning the rededication of the Temple to Jewish use.

In fact the story of *Chanukah* has no source in the Bible – it is told in the Books of the Maccabees, which did not become part of the Hebrew canon. The story in these books, however, has the notable omission of the miracle oil. Thus it could be that *Chanukah* was actually the attempt to recreate *Sukkot*, which the Jewish warriors had been unable to celebrate because of their situation.

The story of the long-lasting oil comes up at last in the later Rabbinic material of Talmudic times. It could be that the shift towards spiritualizing the story was a way of demythologizing the Maccabees, who later themselves became Hellenized and stood against the traditional Rabbis. It was also thought diplomatic not to emphasize a story of Jewish victory over a political overlord while living, as the Rabbis were, under the Romans.

Today *Chanukah* retains some gestures towards victory over oppressive military force. The traditional song sung after the candles are lit, actually composed in the thirteenth century, is to do with this theme. In the Middle Ages the festival also commemorated various acts of martyrdom by Jews who were put to death for refusing to commit sacrilege. Nowadays, though, such gloomy associations have virtually disappeared and *Chanukah* is a cheerful festival which has grown to overlap with the general festivities of the season. It is the most gift-orientated of all the Jewish holidays. While it is customary to give little gifts at other times, *Chanukah* has special associations with chocolate 'gold', sweets and increasingly elaborate present-giving. It is also a time for children's games, traditionally played with spinning tops. While it is often seen as 'the Jewish Christmas', *Chanukah* is really a minor festival, with its own spiritual links. As at *Purim*, it is important to remember that God had a part to play in Jewish redemption – it did not happen through military might alone.

The candles are part of this spiritual message. On each evening of *Chanukah* one more candle is lit on the *chanukiah*, one for the first night, two on the second, and so on until all eight are alight. Each candle is lit by a 'master' candle which stands in the centre. Originally there was some controversy between two Rabbinic schools of thought as to whether the festival should start with eight lights and decline, or the other way round. The system of adding to the lights won the day. The lights start at the right and move leftwards – so the balance of your 'light' is always towards the side of the 'right'.

Even more in keeping with the festival is to use oil rather than candles. Some people fill small glass holders with olive oil and light a wick in each. The *chanukiah* itself is a recognizably Jewish artefact and subject to much artistic endeavour to produce unusual ones.

Having eight candles is of special esoteric significance. The Temple had to undergo seven days of cleansing and purification before it could be dedicated on the eighth day. Firstborn animals were consecrated to God eight days after being born and circumcision takes place on the eighth day after the birth. The number eight is mystically a gateway to the next level – beyond the completion of seven. Eight therefore has something about it of the eternal world, and the Hasidim celebrate the eighth day of *Chanukah* with especial rejoicing. Each light can show us how the light of the Sanctuary can still be within our homes and our souls, even at the darkest time. The *Chanukah* lights are supposed to be set in a window or doorway where they can be seen. Their subtle illumination is a way of encouraging light in the depths of darkness, without the brash gaudiness that usually attends the time of year.

SIMCHAT TORAH – REJOICING OF THE LAW

The Rejoicing of the Law follows immediately on from *Sukkot*, with an interconnecting yet distinct festival between them. That is *Shemini Atzeret*, the Eighth Day of Solemn Assembly. In Temple times it was probably one extra day after *Sukkot* on which pilgrims stayed in Jerusalem, or, more mystically, regarded as an extra day on which God asked his people to stay close to him. There are no real rituals required – it was simply an extra holiday on which a prayer for winter rainfall was made. Since the date was also that of the annual completion of the reading of the *Torah*, it also began to be a celebration of that occasion.

In the Diaspora *Shemini Atzeret* is the eighth day of *Sukkot*, but in Israel it is also *Simchat Torah*. *Simchat Torah* does, however, have its own special characteristics. Marking the end and the beginning of the *Torah* readings, it is a time of festivity and rejoicing. Like *Purim*, its celebration is often left to children, but orthodox communities have a night of singing and dancing for the whole community. Hasidic communities, especially, dance in close groups of men, circling around the Ark with a *Torah* scroll.

On the morning of the festival, children are especially encouraged to participate. A prayer shawl is spread over the heads of all children present and a special blessing said over them. Although the festival is likened to *Purim* because of the riotous nature of its celebrations, it has a different feel to it. Full honour is given to the *Torah* scrolls, the word of God.

Simchat Torah also has a sense of completion and of renewal. It marks the conclusion of relating the spiritual story of the Jewish people and also the commitment to beginning a new cycle of relationship with that living tradition. It is the end of the cycle of the main holy days of the Jewish year, which have occurred in a continuous pattern through the autumn. It brings in a dimension linked to land and nature, speaking of seasonal change and the desire that the Earth and everything on it should flourish. It is a time for relief and forgiveness, and building a life founded in peace, well-being and the rejoicing of the heart.

GLOSSARY OF
HEBREW TERMS

Hebrew words used only once or twice are explained as part of the text. Here is a list of more frequently used terms.

Ashkenazi Hebrew name for 'German', but later denoting Jewish people and culture which spread westwards from the Middle East to Italy, France and Germany.

Halacha Jewish law.

Hasidism from 'pious', originally appertaining to a group of medieval German Jewish pietists but now more generally taken to mean the movement started in the middle of the 18th century by Jews adhering to especially rigorous practices in order to experience more fully their inner meaning.

Kabbalah literally 'reception'. Now taken as meaning the Jewish mystical tradition, in particular from medieval times onwards.

Kabbalist one who is involved in Jewish mystical practices.

Kashrut Jewish dietary laws.

Mitzvot commands of God followed by observant Jews.

Sephardi Oriental or Eastern Jews and Jewish culture, later also spreading to Spain, Portugal and North Africa.

Sefirot the originating cosmic forces involved in the creation of the universe, also aspects of God.

Shabbat Saturday, the Jewish Sabbath.

Shekhinah originally the dwelling place of God on earth, later the feminine aspect of God.

Talmud the written text, originating in Rabbinic times, of what was once the oral tradition of Jewish law and practice.

Torah the first five books of the Bible.

BIBLIOGRAPHY

INTRODUCTION

Martin Buber, *I and Thou*, Edinburgh, 1984
—, *The Way of Response*
Arthur Green (ed.), *Jewish Spirituality from the Bible through the Middle Ages*, London, 1986
Gloria Karpinski, *Where Two Worlds Touch*, London, 1991
Zalman Schachter-Shalomi with David Gropman, *The First Step: A Guide for the New Jewish Spirit*, New York, 1983

CHAPTER 1: IN THE PRESENCE OF GOD

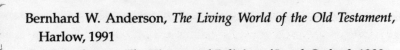

Bernhard W. Anderson, *The Living World of the Old Testament*, Harlow, 1991
G. W. Anderson, *The History and Religion of Israel*, Oxford, 1989
Karen Armstrong, *A History of Jerusalem*, London, 1996
Eli Barnavi (ed.), *A Historical Atlas of the Jewish People*, London, 1994
John Bright, *A History of Israel*, London, 1991
David Daiches, *Moses: Man in the Wilderness*, London, 1975
Roland de Vaux, *The Early History of Israel*, London, 1978
—, *Ancient Israel: Its Life and Institutions*, London, 1991
Jerry M. Landay, *The House of David*, London, 1973

CHAPTER 2: THE COVENANT IN ACTION

Eli Barnavi (ed.), *A Historical Atlas of the Jewish People*, London, 1994

H. H. Ben-Sasson (ed.), *A History of the Jewish People*, Tel Aviv, 1969

David R. Blumenthal, *Understanding Jewish Mysticism: The Merkabah Tradition and the Zoharic Tradition*, New York, 1978

Ben Zion Bokser, *The Jewish Mystical Tradition*, Northvale, New Jersey, 1993

Peter Brown, *The World of Late Antiquity*, London, 1991

Arthur Green (ed.), *Jewish Spirituality from the Bible through the Middle Ages*, London, 1986

Robert M. Seltzer (ed.), *Judaism: A People and its History*, New York, 1989

Gershom Scholem, *The Messianic Idea in Judaism*, New York, 1971

Hershel Shanks (ed.), *Christianity and Rabbinic Judaism*, London, 1993

Geza Vermes, *The Dead Sea Scrolls in English*, London, 1990

CHAPTER 3: MEDIEVAL SPIRITUALITY

David Ariel, *The Mystic Quest*, New York, 1988

Eli Barnavi (ed.), *A Historical Atlas of the Jewish People*, London, 1994

H. H. Ben-Sasson (ed.), *A History of the Jewish People*, Tel Aviv, 1969

Robert Chazan, *European Jewry and the First Crusade*, Berkeley, 1987

Lawrence Fine (trans. and intro.), *Safed Spirituality*, Mahwah, New Jersey, 1984

Louis Finkelstein, *Rab Saadia Gaon: Studies in his Honour*, New York, 1944

Marvin Fox, *Interpreting Maimonides*, Chicago, 1990

Isaac Husik, *A History of Medieval Jewish Philosophy*, Philadelphia, 1944

Moshe Idel, *Kabbalah: New Perspectives*, Yale, 1988

—, *The Mystical Experience in Abraham Abulafia*, New York, 1988

—, *Studies in Ecstatic Kabbalah*, New York, 1988

Aryeh Kaplan (trans., intro.), *The Bahir*, Maine, 1979

—, *Sefer Yetsirah*, York Beach, Maine, 1993

Jacob Katz, *Exclusiveness and Tolerance*, New Jersey, 1961

David Knowles, *The Evolution of Medieval Thought*, Harlow, Essex, 1988

Moses Maimonides, *The Guide of the Perplexed*, Chicago and London, 1963

Ivan Marcus, *Piety and Society*, Leiden, 1981

David Chanan Matt (trans.), *Zohar: The Book of Enlightenment*, Ramsey, New Jersey, 1983

Simon Noveck (ed.), *Creators of the Jewish Experience*, Washington, DC, 1985

Gershom Scholem, *Major Trends in Jewish Mysticism*, New York, 1974

— (ed.), *Zohar, The Book of Splendour*, New York, 1977

—, *Origins of the Kabbalah*, Princeton, 1987

Colette Sirat, *A History of Jewish Philosophy in the Middle Ages*, Cambridge, 1985

CHAPTER 4: TOWARDS TODAY

Dean Ben-Amos and Jerome R. Mintz (trans. and ed.), *In Praise of the Baal Shem Tov*, Northvale, New Jersey, 1993

H. H. Ben-Sasson (ed.), *A History of the Jewish People*, Tel Aviv, 1969

Martin Buber, *On Zion*, New York, 1973

Israel Cohen, *A Short History of Zionism*, London, 1951

Lucy S. Dawidowicz, *The Golden Tradition*, New York, 1984

Max Dimont, *The Indestructible Jews*, New York, 1973

Arthur Herzberg (ed.), *The Zionist Idea*, New York, 1966

Theodor Herzl, *Old-New Land*, Haifa, 1961

Abraham J. Heschel, *The Circle of the Baal Shem Tov*, Chicago and London, 1985

Gershom David Hundert (ed.), *Essential Papers on Hasidism*, New York and London, 1991

Moshe Idel, *Hasidism, Between Ecstasy and Magic*, Albany, 1995

Jacob Katz, *Out of the Ghetto*, New York, 1978

Howard Morley Sacher, *The Course of Modern Jewish History*, New York, 1977

Rivka Schatz Uffenheimer, *Hasidism as Mysticism*, Jerusalem, 1993

Joseph Weiss, *Studies in Eastern European Jewish Mysticism*, Oxford, 1985

CHAPTER 5: PRAYER AND RITUAL

Hayim Halevy Donin, *To Pray as a Jew*, USA, 1980

Louis Jacobs, *Hasidic Prayer*, London, 1993

—, *The Jewish Religion: A Companion*, Oxford, 1995

Yehudah Lebovits and Mordechai Rosen, *With an Eye on Eternity*, Jerusalem, 1994

Jonathan Wittenberg, *Three Pillars of Judaism*, London, 1966

CHAPTER 6: BIRTH AND DEATH

David Ariel, *What do Jews Believe?*, London, 1996

Louis Jacobs, *The Book of Jewish Belief*, New York, 1984

Aryeh Kaplan, *Inner Space*, Jerusalem, 1989

Jack Riemer (ed.), *Jewish Insights on Death and Mourning*, New York, 1995

Zalman Schachter-Shalomi with David Gropman, *The First Step: A Guide for the New Jewish Spirit*, New York, 1983

CHAPTER 7: RELATIONSHIP AND INTIMACY

David Biale, *Eros and the Jews*, New York, 1992
Shmuley Boteach, *Kosher Sex*, London, 1999
Abraham Cohen, *Everyman's Talmud*, New York, 1949
Hayim Halevy Donin, *To Be a Jew*, USA, 1972
Blu Greenberg, *On Women and Judaism*, Philadelphia, 1996
Ruth K. Westheimer and Jonathan Mark, *Heavenly Sex*, New York and London, 1995

CHAPTER 8: WORK AND REST

Yechiel Bar Lev, *Song for the Sabbath*, Petach Tikva, 1994
Hayim Halevy Donin, *To Be a Jew*, USA, 1972
Louis Jacobs, *The Book of Jewish Belief*, New York, 1984
Alan Unterman, *Jews*, Boston, London, Henley-on-Thames, 1981

CHAPTER 9: EATING AND DRINKING

David Ariel, *What Do Jews Believe?*, London, 1996
Abraham Cohen, *Everyman's Talmud*, New York, 1949
Hayim Halevy Donin, *To Be a Jew*, USA, 1972
Louis Jacobs, *The Book of Jewish Belief*, New York, 1984
Dennis Prager and Joseph Telushkin, *The Nine Questions People Ask about Judaism*, New York, 1986
Claudia Roden, *The Book of Jewish Food*, Great Britain, 1997

Isaac N. Fabricant, *A Guide to Succoth*, London, 1969
Isaac Levy, *A Guide to Passover*, London, 1969
Chaim Pearl, *A Guide to Shavuoth*, London, 1969
Chaim Raphael, *A Feast of History*, London, 1984
Michael Strassfield, *The Jewish Holidays*, New York, 1985

CHAPTER 11: FASTS

David Ariel, *The Mystic Quest*, New York, 1988
Louis Jacobs, *A Guide to Yom Kippur*, London, 1969
—, *The Book of Jewish Belief*, New York, 1984
Chaim Pearl, *A Guide to the Minor Festivals and Fasts*, London, 1969
Michael Strassfield, *The Jewish Holidays*, New York, 1985

CHAPTER 12: RENEWALS

Jeffrey M. Cohen, *Understanding the High Holyday Services*, London, 1983
Louis Jacobs, *A Guide to Rosh Hashanah*, London, 1969
Chaim Pearl, *A Guide to the Minor Festivals and Fasts*, London, 1969
Michael Strassfield, *The Jewish Holidays*, New York, 1985

CHAPTER 13: CARNIVALS, LIGHTS AND REJOICING

Louis Jacobs, *The Jewish Religion: A Companion*, Oxford, 1995
S. M. Lehrman, *A Guide to Hanukkah and Purim*, London, 1969
Michael Strassfield, *The Jewish Holidays*, New York, 1985